Raymund Harris

Scriptural researches on the licitness of the slave-trade

shewing its conformity with the principles of natural and revealed religion,

delineated in the sacred writings of the Word of God

Raymund Harris

Scriptural researches on the licitness of the slave-trade
shewing its conformity with the principles of natural and revealed religion,
delineated in the sacred writings of the Word of God

ISBN/EAN: 9783744742047

Printed in Europe, USA, Canada, Australia, Japan

Cover: Foto ©ninafisch / pixelio.de

More available books at **www.hansebooks.com**

SCRIPTURAL RESEARCHES

ON THE LICITNESS

OF THE

SLAVE - TRADE,

SHEWING ITS CONFORMITY

WITH THE PRINCIPLES OF

NATURAL AND REVEALED RELIGION,

DELINEATED IN THE

SACRED WRITINGS OF THE WORD OF GOD.

BY THE REV. R. HARRIS.

SEARCH THE SCRIPTURES, FOR IN THEM YE THINK YE HAVE
ETERNAL LIFE. JOHN. C. 5. V. 39.

LIVERPOOL:

PRINTED BY H. HODGSON, POOL-LANE,

M.DCC.LXXXVIII.

T O

The Worshipful the MAYOR,

RECORDER, ALDERMEN, BAILIFFS,

And other Members of the Common Council

Of the ancient and loyal BOROUGH and

CORPORATION of LIVERPOOL,

The following Scriptural Researches

On the licitnefs of the SLAVE-TRADE,

Are moft refpectfully infcribed

BY

Their moft obedient

And moft humble Servant,

RAYMUND HARRIS.

P R E F A C E.

UNWILLING to incur the difpleafure of every friend to juftice, religion, and humanity, I haften to inform the Reader, who has caft an eye on the Title-page, that, in attempting to eftablifh the licitnefs of the SLAVE-TRADE, nothing is farther removed from my thoughts, than to fet up as an advocate for injuftice and oppreffion: I am as much at enmity with both, as the moft fanguine advocate for African Liberty may be. I am well apprized, that acts of violence and oppreffion, however authorized by numbers, however firmly eftablifhed by long ufe, and a kind of traditional inattention to the fufferings of perfons in an abject condition of life, can never change the criminality of their nature. Whatever is effentially incompatible with the facred and inalienable rights of juftice and humanity, can claim no place in the catalogue of virtues, even of the loweft rank; it muft be for ever branded with every mark of infamy and guilt.

FAR then from attempting the leaft encroachment on the rights of Virtue, my fole drift in the prefent Tract is to examine with the utmoft impartiality, the intrinfic nature of the SLAVE-TRADE: that is, whether the Trade itfelf, prefcinding from every other incidental circumftance, which may have rendered the practice of it hateful, or even criminal, be in its own nature licit or illicit.

Now, it being evident in the firft place, that the intrinfic morality or immorality, licitnefs or illicitnefs of all human purfuits is effentially inherent to the
purfuits

purfuits themfelves, and not at all depending on our habits or ideas of *Right* and *Wrong*, which are but too often influenced and darkened by prejudice, intereft, and other paffions; and, it being equally evident on the other hand, that the declarations of the Written Word of God are fo many incontrovertible decifions, by which we are to judge of the intrinfic licitnefs or illicitnefs of fuch facts as are regiftered in the Sacred Volumes; it follows neceffarily, that, one of thofe facts being undoubtedly the SLAVE-TRADE, no arguments can be fo forcible and conclufive, towards evincing the inherent lawfulnefs of it, as thofe Oracular decifions of the Word of God, which give a pofitive fanction to the Trade itfelf.—It is then by enforcing thefe unerring decifions only, the fureft guide to direct our judgements in forming a juft eftimate of the merits of the prefent Controverfy, that I mean to vindicate the licitnefs of the SLAVE-TRADE; not by pratronizing fuch crying enormities and abufes, as are faid to be perpetrated in this moft ancient commercial purfuit.

SHOULD the fanction of divine authority appear evident in favour of the SLAVE-TRADE, from the teftimonies I fhall produce in the feries of my Refearches, I fhall confider myfelf perfectly difingaged from the moft diftant obligation of anfwering fuch objections, as are not grounded on the fame divine authority: an authority of that irrefiftible weight of conviction, that every perfon, who has any pretenfions to Religion, muft immediately affent to, however plaufible or ingenious the oppofite arguments may appear, when viewed through the fcanty light of mere human reafon and fenfe.

THE fcope of the following Refearches being evidently to try the merits of the prefent Controverfy by the Sacred Canons of the Written Word of God,

God, I can expect conviction only from such perfons, as are not fo far deftitute of every fentiment
of religion and good fenfe, as to difbelieve the divine authenticity of thofe Sacred Writings, in which
the Finger of God has left in indelible characters
the vifible impreffion of his Wifdom.

Now, as thefe Sacred Records contain tranfactions relative to the Slave-Trade, as practifed in all
the three religious Difpenfations that have appear-
ed in the World fince the formation of the firft of
men to the prefent time, I fhall, accordingly, di-
vide my Scriptural Refearches on that Trade, into
three feparate Parts : in which I fhall fucceffively
prove, that the Slave-Trade is perfectly confonant to the principles of the Law of Nature, the
Mofaic Difpenfation, and the Chriftian Law, as delineated to us in the Sacred Writings of the Word
of God.

I have prefixed to the whole a few pofitions or
Data, which, I truft, will be found unqueftionably
true, and exactly conformable to found reafon ; in
order, that I may not be interrupted in the fequel with
unneceffary repetitions of general principles, nor
be in the leaft conftrained to enter into a formal con-
futation of arguments, which do not immediately
affect my fubject, and that the Reader may fee at
one view the very fundamental principles of thofe
inferences, which I draw in vindication of the Slave-
Trade from the Scriptural paffages I have felected in
the courfe of my Refearches, out of a greater number of the fame import I could eafily pioduce.

The Scriptural paffages are literally tranfcribed
from the Proteftant Vulgar Tranflation of the Bible ;
which, being the moft generally received in thefe
Kingdoms, will, of courfe, have a greater weight of
authority than any other with the major part of my
Readers.

Readers. The Edition I ufe is that which was pu-
blifhed in London by John Bill and Chriftopher Bar-
ker in the year 1659.

WITH refpect to compofition, I can pretend to
neither elegance nor ftyle : a Foreigner, unacquainted
with the leaft element of the Englifh Language till
the twenty feventh year of his age, can have no claim
to either : if he can but arrange his periods with
a tolerable degree of grammatical accuracy, and exprefs himfelf with fufficient clearnefs, method, and
perfpicuity, he has reafon to expect every indulgence
from the native candour of an Englifh Critic.

D A T A.

D A T A.

I.

THAT the Volume of the Sacred Writings, commonly called the HOLY BIBLE, comprehending both the Old and the New Teſtaments, contains the unerring Deciſions of the Word of God.

II.

THAT theſe Deciſions are of equal authority in both the Teſtaments, and that that authority is the eſſential veracity of God, who is TRUTH itſelf.

III.

THAT, as there can be no preſcription againſt the authority of God, whatever is declared in any part of the Scriptural Records to be intrinſically good or bad, licit or illicit, muſt be eſſentially ſo in its own nature, however contrary any ſuch declaration may be to the received opinions of men for any length of time.

IV.

THAT, as the Supreme Legiſlator of the World is infinitely juſt and wiſe in all his deciſions reſpecting *Right* and *Wrong*, and is no ways accountable to his creatures for the reaſons of his conduct in the government of the World; ſo it muſt be a degree of preſumption highly criminal in any creature to refuſe aſſent to thoſe Deciſions, only becauſe he cannot comprehend the hidden principles of that impartial juſtice, which characterizes every deciſion of God.

V.

THAT no perſon can be ſuppoſed to acknowledge in fact, that the Holy Scriptures are the infallible

Word

Word of God, unless he acquiesces without reserve
in every scriptural Decision, however incomprehen-
sible the reasons and motives of those Decisions may
be to him.

VI.

THAT every person, who professes to acknowledge the Holy Scriptures to be the unerring Word
of God, must consequently assent to every Scriptural Decision without reserve, only because he believes
them to be the declarations of God; who, being
TRUTH itself, can neither err himself, nor lead any
one into error.

VII.

THAT, if one or more Decisions of the Written
Word of God give a positive sanction to the intrinsic
licitness of any human pursuit (for instance, the SLAVE-
TRADE), whoever professes to believe the incontrovertible veracity of the Written Word of God, essentially incompatible with the least degre of injustice,
must consequently believe the pursuit itself to be intrinsically just and lawful in the stricteft sense of the
word.

VIII.

THAT no advantages whatever attending the prosecution of an unlawful pursuit, nor any abuses whatever committed in the prosecution of a lawful one, can
so far affect the pursuits themselves, as to render the
latter intrinsically criminal, or the former essentially
just.

IX.

THAT, as no private or national advantages whatever can alter the inherent turpitude of a pursuit essentially unlawful; so no arguments whatever, built solely
on the strength of those advantages, will ever justify
the SLAVE TRADE, till the same be proved essentially
just and lawful in its nature.

THAT,

X.

THAT, as no abufes or malepractices whatever, com-mitted in the profecution of a lawful purfuit, can ever alter the intrinfic licitnefs of it; fo no arguments whatever, built folely on the ftrength of thofe abufes, will ever evince the intrinfic deformity of the SLAVE-TRADE, any more than that of any other lawful pur-fuit, where abufes are committed, unlefs the fame be proved effentially unjuft and illicit.

XI.

THAT, if abufes and malepractices, committed in the profecution of a lawful purfuit, can be checked and prevented by Legal Authority, the private and national advantages arifing from that purfuit, and the inconveniencies attending the fuppreffion of it, joined to its intrinfic licitnefs, ought to have a very powerful influence towards not abolifhing the profecution of that purfuit.

XII.

THAT, if abufes and malepractices, though evident-ly fubject to the control of the Legiflature, are to be confidered as fufficient arguments to fupprefs the SLAVE-TRADE, without any regard to its intrinfic licitnefs, every other branch of Trade, in which abufes are committed, ought, on the fame account, to fhare the fame fate.

SECTION.

SECTION I.

Scriptural Researches on the licitness of the Slave-Trade, shewing its conformity with the principles of the Law of Nature delineated in the Sacred Writings.

I. THAT period of years, which elapsed from the day on which *God created Man in his own image* (a), to the day, on which He gave his Laws to the Children of Israel on Mount Sinai (b), is generally called the period of the Law of Nature. The exact duration of this period is a matter of controversy among the Learned. Archbishop Usher, whose chronological accuracy in the computation of scriptural years is much admired, reckons 2513 years between the Creation of the World and the promulgation of the Mosaic Law. But be this as it may (for no difference in computation can affect the subject of my present Researches), it is evident from the tenour of the Sacred Records, that, between the creation of Adam and the promulgation of the Mosaic Law, the Dispensation of the Law of Nature, commonly called Natural Religion, or the Religion of Nature, was the only true Religion in the World.

II. Simple as the principles of this Religion may appear, directed chiefly to worship One, Supreme, Eternal, Being, the Creator and Governor of all things, and to chuse and act in exact conformity to the inward dictates of sound and unbiassed reason in every transaction of life, where *Right* and *Wrong* were left to choice of Man; it would be exceedingly difficult, as well as perfectly extraneous to my present subject, to digest those principles into a regular Code of those
particular

(a) Genesis, c. 1. v, 27.　(b) Exodus, c. 29, &c,

particular laws and duties, which conftituted the whole
fyftem of that Religion.—I have not engaged to dif-
play the whole frame and ftrudure of Natural Religion:
I am to fhew no farther, than that the principles and
laws of that Religion, as far as we find them delineated
in the Sacred Writings, not only never forbade the
SLAVE-TRADE, or hinted the moft diftant oppofition
to the profecution of it; but that, the fame being
frequently exemplified in the conftant and uninterrupted practice of fome of the moft faithful obfervers of
the laws and principles of that Religion, under the
vifible protection of God, whofe favourites they were,
the laws and principles themfelves were in perfect
harmony with the practice of the SLAVE-TRADE.—
Two very fingular inftances of this kind, verified in
the conduct of two of the moft diftinguifhed Characters within the above period of the Law of Nature,
ABRAHAM and JOSEPH, will, I flatter myfelf, be fufficient, without mentioning others, to juftify my affertion, and fet the prefent Controverfy in the cleareft
light of Scriptural conviction.

A B R A H A M.

III. IN every place of Scripture, where mention
is made of this Venerable Patriarch, he is uniformly
reprefented as a perfect pattern of every virtue. The
ftrongeft faith in God (*c*), the firmeft reliance on his
promifes (*d*), and the readieft and moft unreferved
obedience to his commands (*e*); the moft fympathiz-
ing humanity to every fellow-creature (*f*), the ftricteft juftice and integrity in all his dealings with men (*g*)
and the utmoft difintereftednefs of heart (*h*); infine,
the

(*c*) Gen. 15. 6. Rom. 4. 3. Galat. 3. 6. James, 2. 23. (*d*) Ibid.
(*e*) Gen. 22. v. 1—13. (*f*) Gen. 18. 23, &c.
(*g*) Gen. 21. 22, &c. Gen. 23. 7, &c. (*h*) Gen. 14. 22, 23.

[14]

the greatest love of peace and harmony (*i*), together with every other religious, domeſtic, and ſocial virtue (*k*), are the diſtinguiſhing characteriſtics of his perſon.

IV. Owing, no doubt, to theſe exalted virtues, he is frequently repreſented in Scripture in familiar intercourſe with God *(l)*; who, in innumerable places of Holy Writ, ſtyles himſelf emphatically *The God of Abraham*, as the moſt àcceptable perſon he had on earth : he calls him *His Friend* (*m*), and makes the moſt exalted panegyric of his virtues, when, appearing to his ſon Iſaac after the death of his Father, he ſpeaks to him in the following remarkable and comprehenſive words : *In thy ſeed ſhall all the nations of the earth be bleſſed; becauſe that Abraham obeyed my voice, and kept my charge, my commandments, my ſtatutes, and my laws* (*n*).

V. Nor is his unimpeachable character, as a righteous man, leſs conſpicuous in the Writings of the New Teſtament; where, among many other teſtimonies of his irreproachable life, the Son of God himſelf, who always ſpeaks of him as one of the moſt faithful ſervants of his Eternal Father, rebukes the Jews for having ſo far departed from the rectitude of Abraham's conduct, as not to be entitled to the appellation of his Children ; for, *If ye were Abraham's children*, ſays he, *ye would do the works of Abraham* (*o*).

VI. Now, it is very remarkable, that among the *works* of Abraham, the very faithful, obedient, humane, juſt, diſintereſted, righteous, and virtuous Abraham, who conſtantly obeyed the voice of God, kept his charge, his commandments, his ſtatutes, and his
laws

(*i*) Gen. 21. 22, &c. Gen. 13. 7, &c. (*k*) Gen. 18. 19.
(*l*) Gen. 12. 1, &c. Gen. 15. 1, &c. Gen. 17. 1, &c. Gen. 18. 1, &c.
(*m*) Iſaiah, 41. 8. (*n*) Gen. 26. 4, 5. (*o*) John, 8. 39,

laws, and found such acceptance with him, as to be admitted to the familiarity of his friendly intercourse; it is very remarkable, I say, that there should be found among his *works* the practice of dealing in human flesh, the practice of purchasing with money those of his own species, and making them *Bond-Slaves* (*p*), without the least intimation being ever given by any of the inspired Writers, that his con- duct in this particular, where the natural rights of justice and humanity are said to be so essentially. inte- rested, was ever reproved, or even discountenanced in the most distant manner by any private or public in- timation of God's displeasure!

VII. And what can we reasonably conclude from this uniform silence of the inspired Writers ? but that the practice of purchasing slaves was never accounted in the sight of God a violation of any of the laws of the Religion of Nature. For, is it credible, or, ra- ther, is it possible for any one to believe, consistently with the ideas we ought to entertain of the infinite holiness of God, in whom dwelleth essentially the ful- ness of justice, that he would style himself *The God of Abraham*, in preference to any other; that he would vouchsafe to honour him with the appellation of *His Friend*; that he would bless in his seed all the nations of the earth (*q*); that he would declare he had obey- ed his voice, kept his charge, his commandments, his statutes, and his laws, without excepting any one; or that Jesus Christ would have ever commended his works without any restriction whatever, if the Slave- Trade, so publickly and so constantly practised by Abraham, had been an iniquitous, unnatural pursuit, essentially opposite to the sacred laws of Nature, to the natural rights of justice and humanity ?

VIII. The

(*p*) Gen. 17. 23, 27.   (*q*) Gen. 22. v. 18.

VIII. The force of this powerful inference, conſidered even as a mere negative argument in favour of the intrinſic licitneſs of the Slave-Trade, carries ſuch an irreſiſtible weight of conviction, that it amounts, in my opinion, to a poſitive approbation of it : it being otherwiſe impoſſible to reconcile the juſtice of God with his own ſcriptural deciſions concerning the eſſential impartiality, and eternal unchangeableneſs of its nature.

IX. That this poſitive approbation, this ſanction of Divine Authority in favour of the Slave-Trade, ſo viſible in the conduct of God, eye-witneſs to every tranſaction of Abraham's life, is not a bare conjecture, or a mere negative inference of a paſſionate advocate for ſlavery, but the real intent and meaning of the Written Word of God, will appear evident to the moſt zealous advocate for African Liberty, who, diveſting himſelf for a moment of every prejudice, that the love of humanity may have created in his mind, will diſpaſſionately examine with me the ſtriking circumſtances of the following Caſe. It is that of a Bond-Slave in the ſervice of Abraham ; which, as related in the Sacred Writings, contains ſuch intereſting particulars, that, I flatter myſelf, it will evince to demonſtration, that the Slave-Trade has the indiſputable ſanction of Divine Authority, even when attended with circumſtances not of the moſt pleaſing complexion to the eyes of humanity.

X. This very deciſive fact is thus literally related in the xvi[th] Chapter of the Book of Genesis.

1. Now Sarai Abram's wife bare him no children : and ſhe had an hand-maid, an Egyptian, whoſe name was Hagar,

2. And Sarai ſaid unto Abram : behold now, the Lord hath reſtrained me from bearing : I pray thee, go in unto my maid : it may be, that I may obtain

obtain children by her : and Abram hearkened to the voice of Sarai.

3. And Sarai Abram's wife took Hagar her maid, the Egyptian, after Abram had dwelt ten years in the land of Canaan, and gave her to her hufband Abram to be his wife.

4. And he went in unto Hagar, and fhe conceived : and when fhe faw that fhe had conceived, her miftrefs was defpifed in her eyes.

5. And Sarai faid unto Abram : my wrong be upon thee : I have given my maid into thy bofom ; and when fhe faw fhe had conceived, I was defpifed in her eyes : the Lord judge between me and thee.

6. But Abram faid unto Sarai : behold, thy maid is in thy hand ; do to her as it pleafeth thee. And when Sarai dealt hardly with her, fhe fled from her face.

7. And the Angel found her by a fountain of water in the wildernefs, by the fountain in the way to Shur.

8. And he faid : Hagar, Sarai's maid, whence comeft thou ? and whither wilt thou go ? And fhe faid : I flee from the face of my miftrefs Sarai.

9. And the Angel of the Lord faid unto her : return unto thy miftrefs, and fubmit thyfelf under her hands.

10. And the Angel of the Lord faid unto her : I will multiply thy feed exceedingly, that it fhall not be numbered for multitude.

11. And the Angel of the Lord faid unto her : behold, thou art with child, and fhalt bear a fon, and fhalt call his name Ifhmael ; becaufe the Lord hath heard thy affliction.

XI. Enough have we for the prefent to obferve on this portion of Hagar's hiftory, without proceeding to relate the treatment fhe received in her Mafter's houfe fome time after her return.— Here we have a

C   Hand-maid,

Hand-maid, called foon after a *Bond-woman* by God himfelf (*r*); born in Africa, for fhe was an Egyptian by birth, and, confequently, an *African Slave*; labouring under every natural difadvantage attending the condition of a Bond-flave; bought by a ftranger, tranfported from her native Country into a diftant land, the Land of Canaan, where Abram dwelt; that is, tranfported from Africa into Afia: feparated for ever from her deareft relations, friends, and acquaintance, and obliged to wait at hand, and work for the advantage of her Mafters.

XII. The fterility of her Miftrefs feemed rather to flatter Hagar with the profpect of meliorating her condition, by becoming her Mafter's wife at the folicitation of her Miftrefs: but the event proved the contrary, and difappointed all her hopes; for not only fhe did not obtain her freedom by becoming his wife, but finding fhe was with child by her Mafter, and being, on this account, not quite fo refpectful to her Miftrefs, as the latter expected in quality of Abram's principal wife, fhe was fo roughly handled by Sarai, with the permiffion of Abram, that, unable to bear her treatment, fhe fled from her houfe, left her fervice, and took refuge in the defert. What the correction was, that Sarai inflicted on Hagar, is not particularly fpecified in the Sacred Hiftory: the Hebrew word ufed upon the occafion, and rendered by the Tranflators *dealt hardly*, has fuch an extent of fignification, as may eafily convey the idea of a very cruel and oppreffive treatment, which, in the actual ftate of Hagar's pregnancy, muft have rendered her affliction much more intolerable and oppreffive.

XIII. Every circumftance attending the wretched fituation of this poor African Slave, who, though legally

gally married to her Mafter, is kept ftill in bondage, and forced, as it were, out of his houfe and fervice in the condition fhe was in, through hard ufage and feverity, though charged with no other crime, but being not quite fo refpectful to her hufband's firft wife as fhe had been before her marriage, feems to excite compaffion, and juftify her efcape.—Were Hagar's cafe that of any African female flave now in the Weft-Indies, and were the fame to be tried before a jury compofed of fome of the prefent advocates for African Liberty in this Ifland, one might decide almoft to a certainty in whofe favour the verdict would be given: the Slave would moft probably be declared free, and both Mafter and Miftrefs feverely reprimanded, if not alfo condemned in a heavy precuniary mulct: no other verdict would be confiftent with the principles they fo publickly avow.

XIV. But did Hagar obtain the fame favourable fentence at the impartial Tribunal of God, when fhe pleaded her Caufe before the Minifter of his juftice, whom he deputed to reprefent his Perfon? Did he approve of her conduct in leaving her Mafter's houfe, and quitting his fervice? Did he hint the moft diftant reflection on the proceedings of Abram or her Miftrefs Sarai? Did he fignify to her, that her quality of Abram's wife, or the feverity of Sarai's treatment, even in her actual ftate of pregnancy, emancipated her from her bondage, refcinded the original contract of her purchafe, or that that contract had been illicit and contrary to his laws, or that fhe might, on this account, confider herfelf as no part of Abram's lawful property, but at full liberty to difpofe of her perfon as fhe thought beft?—NO:—on the contrary, her conduct was condemned by the Reprefentative of God, who ordered her in his name *to return to her Miftrefs, and fubmit herfelf under her hands*; though at the fame

time

time he affured her, that *the Lord had heard her affliction.*

XV. Were all other fcriptural evidences wanted in favour of the Slave-Trade, this Decree alone of the higheft Court of Juftice poffible, this folemn Sentence of the Supreme Judge of *Right* and *Wrong, Who is no refpecter of perfons, but, in every nation, he that feareth him, and worketh righteoufnefs, is accepted with him* (s), and who, in the cafe before us, had an intuitive and comprehenfive knowledge of every particular circumftance attending the claims of both the Parties, muft convince every impartial Reader, that the licitnefs of that Trade is evidently warranted by the Written Word of God; who, by the very act of deputing an Angel, on purpofe to command the fugitive Slave to return to her Mafter's houfe, and fubmit herfelf under the hands of her Miftrefs, declared her to be her Mafter's indifputable property, and the original bargain or contract, by which he had acquired that property, to be juft and lawful in its nature: that is, that the Slave-Trade, even when attended with circumftances not altogether conformable to the feelings of humanity, is effentially confiftent with the facred and inalienable rights of juftice, and has the pofitive fanction of God in its fupport; however difpleafing thofe circumftances may be to his fatherly Providence, as they appear to have been in the Cafe of Hagar; who, in alleviation of her fufferings and affliction, was promifed the honour of being the Mother of a numerous progeny, branched out afterwards into twelve powerful kingdoms (t).

J O S E P H.

XVI. Whoever has the leaft acquaintance with the principal human Characters exhibited in the Sacred
Records,

(s) Acts, c. 10. v. 34, 35. (t) Gen. c. 25. v. 16.

Records, muſt readily acknowledge, that the character
of Joseph, great grand-ſon to Patriarch Abraham, is
one of the moſt amiable, moſt upright, and inſtructive.
He is there repreſented in every viciſſitude of fortune,
acquiring in every ſtation by his wiſdom and virtue
favour with God and man (*u*).   His virtue ſuffers no
diminution whaterer, but ſhines with greater luſtre, in
paſſing from the condition of a ſlave to that of Governor of all Egypt.   His fidelity to God, and to his
Maſter Potiphar, is aſſailed by ſtrong temptations,
which, in ſpite of youth and intereſt, he reſiſts with
the moſt exemplary fortitude (*w*).   Thrown into the
horrors of a dungeon through the artifice of a falſe
woman, whoſe honour he preſerves at the expence of
his own, his integrity and prudence ſoon render him
conſpicuous even in that dark receſs (*x*).   Favoured
with the divine ſpirit of prophecy, and called in his
Prophetic Character into the preſence of Pharaoh, the
wiſe and extenſive plan he forms to ſave the Kingdom
from the miſeries of impending famine, raiſes him to
that height, where his abilities and virtues are eminent-
ly diſplayed in the public ſervice, and anſwer the pur-
poſes of the Providence of God in favour of his choſen People (*y*).   Enabled by deſpotic power to retain
his unnatural brethren in that Egyptian bondage, to
which they had once conſigned him, and gratify revenge by every accumulation of diſgrace, he not only
generouſly forgives them the outrageous treatment he
had received, but he even effaces the very remem-
brance of thoſe injuries which had produced his ad-
verſity:

(*u*) Gen. 39. 2—6.   Ibid. 21—23.   Ibid. c. 41. 37, &c.
(*w*) Gen. 39. 7—12.   (*x*) Gen. 39. 21—23.   Gen. 40. 1, &c.
(*y*) Gen. 40. 8—23.   Ibid. c. 41. 1, &c.   Ibid. c. 45, 4, &c.
Pſ. 105. 16—24.

verfity; and, without recriminating his adverfaries, without retaliating their injuries, he extenuates in fome meafure the guilt of a crime, which, by the interpofition of Providence, had proved fubfervient to a happy iffue (z).

XVII. Every feature of this moft amiable Character is fo perfectly finifhed, fo exactly conformable to the model of the ftricteft virtue, that the whole Piece is one of the completeft portraits of righteoufnefs and humanity, that has ever been exhibited to the World in any ftage of Religion. Chriftianity itfelf can produce but few exemplars, that will contend with him for fuperiority; efpecially, when it is confidered, that Jofeph's innocence and virtue, from his youth to his decrepit old age, retained, in the very heart of infidelity itfelf, the fame uniform luftre and firmnefs, though befet at different periods by fuch ftrong temptations to infidelity and vice, as are the infeparable attendants of extreme adverfity and profperity. In a word: every ftep of Jofeph's conduct in every ftage of his life met the approbation of God, and was efpecially directed by his protecting hand; for, in the language of the infpired Writer, *The Lord was with him: and that which he did, the Lord made it to profper (a).*

XVIII. Now, if we examine the hiftory of this eminent Perfonage, as defcribed in the Sacred Records, we fhall foon find a fecond very remarkable inftance of the licitnefs of the SLAVE-TRADE, as practifed, not only without control, but under the vifible protection of God, by one of the ftricteft profeffors of the Religion of Nature, the laws and principles of which were the invariable rule of his conduct: a man in high favour with the Almighty, the framer of thofe very principles and laws; and who, in the infcrutable or-

der

(z) Gen. c. 37. 23—28. Ibid. 45. 1—11. (a) Gen. 39. 23.

der of his fatherly Providence, chofe him the inftru-
ment and promoter of his glory (*b*), imparted him the
divine fpirit of his wifdom (*c*), led him, as it were, by
the hand, in every ftep of his life (*d*), and profpered
whatever he undertook (*e*). An inftance, attended
with circumftances of that fingular nature and tenden-
cy, as feems not only to fix the fubject of the prefent
Controverfy in the beft point of view, but to afcer-
tain, beyond the power of reply, the inherent lawfulnefs of the Slave-Trade.

XIX. The fact, with all its attending circumftances,
is thus defcribed in the XLVII th Chapter of the Book
of Genesis.

13. And there was no bread in all the land; for the
famine was very fore: fo that the land of Egypt,
and the land of Canaan fainted by reafon of the
famine.

14. And Jofeph gathered up all the money that was
found in the land of Egypt, and in the land of Canaan, for the corn which they brought; and Jofeph
brought the money into Pharaoh's houfe.

15. And when the money failed in the land of Egypt,
and in the land of Canaan, all the Egyptians came
unto Jofeph, and faid: give us bread; for why
fhould we die in thy prefence? for the money faileth.

16. And Jofeph faid: give your cattle; and I will
give you for your cattle, if money fail.

17. And they brought their cattle unto Jofeph: and
Jofeph gave them bread in exchange for horfes, and
for the flocks, and for the cattle of the herds, and for
the affes; and he fed them with bread for all their
cattle, for that year.

18. When

(*b*) Pf. 105. 16—24. (*c*) Gen. c. 40. 43. (*d*) Gen. 39, 21—23.
(*e*) Gen. 39. 23.

18. When that year was ended, they came unto him the fecond year, and faid unto him: we will not hide it from my Lord, how that our money is fpent; my Lord alfo hath our herds of cattle; there is not aught left in the fight of my Lord, but our bodies and our lands.

19. Wherefore fhall we die before thine eyes, both we and our land? Buy us and our land for bread, and we and our land will be fervants unto Pharaoh: and give us feed, that we may live and not die, that the land be not defolate.

20. And Jofeph bought all the land of Egypt for Pharaoh: for the Egyptians fold every man his field; becaufe the famine prevailed over them: fo the land became Pharaoh's.

21. And as for the people, he removed them to cities, from one end of the borders of Egypt, even unto the other end thereof.

22. Only the land of the Priefts bought he not; for the Priefts had a portion affigned them of Pharaoh, and did eat their portion which Pharaoh gave them; wherefore they fold not their lands.

23. Then Jofeph faid unto the people: behold, I have bought you this day, and your land for Pharaoh: lo, here is feed for you, and ye fhall fow the land.

24. And it fhall come to pafs in the encreafe, that ye fhall give the fifth part unto Pharaoh, and four parts fhall be your own, for feed of the field, and for your food, and for them of your houfholds, and for food for your little ones.

25. And they faid; thou haft faved our lives: let us find grace in the fight of my Lord, and we will be Pharaoh's fervants.

26. And Jofeph made it a law over the land of Egypt unto this day, that Pharaoh fhould have the fifth part;

part; except the land of the Priests only, which became not Pharaoh's.

XX. The transactions related in this portion of Joseph's history, afford us a confiderable number of very pertinent reflections on the Slave-Trade : the following appear to me very remarkable.

1. Here is a whole Nation of free and independent Africans, one only defcription of men excepted, inhabiting the richeft, the moft populous, and the moft civilized part of Africa, or, perhaps, of any other part of the Globe at that period, all made Slaves in one day by a moft explicit, deliberate, and formal contract.

2. Allowing, the Kingdom of Egypt at that time to have extended no farther than it does at prefent; that is, 600 miles from North to South, and 250 from Eaft to Weft, it muft have contained, on the moft moderate computation, as many inhabitants, at leaft, as the Kingdom of Great Britain does at this prefent time; Egypt was then the Emporium of the whole world, where all arts and fciences, commerce, agriculture, and polity flourifhed in a degree of perfection and refinement, fuperior, perhaps, to that of any part of Europe in our days. Accordingly, the number of Africans purchafed by Jofeph in one day, at the very moderate price of one year's maintenance per head, including their land, amounted, at leaft, to feven or eight millions of perfons : a number not unequal, perhaps, to all the purchafes of the kind ever made by Englifh Merchants fince the commencement of the Guinea-Trade.

3. The happy condition of thefe Africans, prior to Jofeph's purchafe, is a circumftance worth obferving : it differed in every refpect from that of moft of their prefent countrymen purchafed by our European Merchants. The latter are generally Slaves, or Cap-

D   tives,

tives, in their native land; the former were all free and independent fubjects: thofe, when purchafed by our African Merchants are in a ftate of abfolute indigence and poverty; whereas the latter were all people of property, and, indeed, of landed property; for it is very particularly fpecified in the fcriptural account that *the Egyptians fold every man his field*; that is, his landed eftate.

4. The circumftance of tranfporting Slaves from their native foil into a diftant Country, is alfo very obvious in the conduct of Jofeph, fubfequent to the purchafe he had made; for, *as for the people*, fays the Scripture, *he removed them to cities, from one end of the borders of Egypt, even unto the other end thereof*: by which expedient he deprived them of every profpect of ever re-enjoying their refpective paternal Eftates, and the places of their nativity. And is it not more than probable, that, in the execution of fo extenfive a plan, as removing fo many millions of inhabitants of every age, fex, condition, and rank, infants at the breaft, young children, old and decrepit people, infirm and delicate, from one end of the borders of fo extenfive a Country as Egypt, even unto the other end thereof, many muft have inevitably perifhed in paffing through the fcorching fands of a Country defolate with famine, and parched up, as it were, by an uninterrupted drought of fix confecutive years, whatever wife regulations we may naturally fuppofe were made by Jofeph to accommodate fuch an extraordinary number of Slaves?

5. This numerous multitude of free and independent Africans, become now by contract menial Slaves to Pharaoh, are immediately fent by Jofeph to cultivate their Mafter's Eftates throughout all Egypt, for *the land became Pharaoh*'s: fo, that we may confider them with the utmoft propriety, as fo many Slaves,

tranfported

tranſported from their native place, and ſent by their Maſter, or his Steward or Overſeer, to work in his different Plantations, merely for their keep; for all the land was the property of Pharaoh, and the portion of the yearly produce of it, which they were allowed, is ſaid to have been given them only *for ſeed of the field, for their food, thoſe of their houſholds, and their little ones.*

6. The laſt and moſt intereſting circumſtance, in my opinion, attending this ſingular tranſaction, is the manner in which Joſeph proceeded to effect his pur-chaſe. For, in conſequence of that prophetic ſpirit, with which the Almighty had eſpecially favoured him, and by which he foreſaw the wonderful fertility of the land for ſeven years to come, and the extreme ſterility of it for as many years after, he engroſſed all the corn that grew in Egypt during the firſt ſeven years of plenty, and laid it up againſt the time of impending famine *(f)*. When this began to rage in the Land, he opened his ſtores, and made the Egyptians pay ready money for their corn : being entirely drained of caſh, for *Joſeph gathered up all the money, that was found in the land of Egypt,* he refuſed to ſupply them with bread, unleſs they gave all their cattle in exchange; which, accordingly, they did, for ſuch proportion of corn as would keep them one year : being now re-duced to the laſt extremity, and entirely deſtitute of proviſions, as well as of every means of procuring them, ſave their lands and perſons, he availed him-ſelf of this favourable opportunity to effect a purchaſe, for which he had gradually paved the way : a bargain was accordingly concluded between him and Pharaoh's ſubjects, by which he bought all their lands and perſons for as much corn, as would keep the latter

D 2   the

(f) Gen. c. 41. v. 47, 49, 55, 56.

the fpace of one year; which, from the circumftance of giving them feed, wherewith to fow the land, appears to have been the laft of that feptennial dearth. So, that, even taking advantage of the extreme indigence of his fellow-creatures, when able to relieve them, in order to reduce them to the condition of Slaves, was not deemed by this righteous, and infpired Man, *with whom the Lord was,* an infraction of thofe facred laws of Nature, which were the invariable rule of his conduct.

XXI. How far Jofeph's conduct in every ftage of this remarkable tranfaction, fo favourable to the Slave-Trade, may appear equitable or otherwife to the prefent humane advocates for African Liberty, through the feeble light of mere human reafon and fenfe, I know not: this however is moft certain, that there is not fo much as one Jot in the Sacred Writings of the Word of God, that feems to difapprove in the moft diftant manner any one part of his conduct, either in this or in any other tranfaction of his long and holy life (g). On the contrary, in every place of Scripture, where this eminent Perfonage is introduced, whether before or after this tranfaction, he is conftantly reprefented as one of the moft faithful and acceptable fervants of God, under whofe particular protection he lived and thrived (h); by whofe immediate direction he acted (i); and who did nothing whatever, but the Almighty *made it to profper* (k). The very tranfaction, we are fpeaking of, when rehearfed by one of the infpired Writers (l), a Man according to God's own heart (m), is fo far from
being

<hr>

(g) Gen. 50. 26. (h) Gen. 39. 21, 23.
(i) Gen. ibid, and cc. 40. 41. (k) Gen. 39. 23. (l) Pf. 105. v. 16—24.
(m) 1. Kings, c. 15. 3.

being taxed with the leaft intimation of guilt in any one circumftance attending it, that the whole pro-cefs, without any exceptions whatever, is there repre-fented as the effect of that divine Wifdom, with which he was infpired from above.

XXII. A FURTHER fcriptural evidence, that the conduct of Jofeph in purchafing fo many millions of his fellow-creatures, and reducing them to the condi-tion of Slaves, met the entire approbation of God, and was therefore perfectly confonant to the facred laws of Nature, is that remarkable declaration of the Word of God, regiftered in the Firft Book of CHRO-NICLES, c. 5. v. 1—3, which affigns the true reafon for transferring the right of Primogeniture, or Firft-born, from the Family of Reuben, eldeft fon of Jacob, to the Family of Jofeph; which, as it is exprefsly mentioned in that place, was Reuben's inceftuous converfation with Bilhah, his Father's concubine (n).—But is it credible, confiftently with the effential juftice of God, that he fhould deprive Reuben's children of their Pri-mogeniture or birth-right, for having once tranfgreffed one of the Laws of Nature, and yet fhould at the fame time, even in preference to Judah the Meffiah's pro-genitor, give it to thofe of Jofeph, who, by the very act of enflaving fo many millions of his fellow-creatures, and ufing them as he did, muft have neceffarily in-curred the horrid guilt of reiterated tranfgreffions of feveral of thofe facred Laws, if, what is fo confidently afferted be true, that the SLAVE-TRADE, or the pur-chafing of Slaves, is an iniquitous unnatural purfuit, and a crime of the blackeft die in direct oppofition to every principle of Nature? How could any one in fuch chimerical fuppofition reconcile the vifible partiality

(n) Gen. 35. 22.

tiality of God's conduct with his own Scriptural declarations of the eternal and immutable rectitude of his
juſtice ?

XXIII. One evidence more, drawn from the ſame
ſcriptural ſource of conviction, will, I hope, be ſufficient to evince the irreproachableneſs of Joſeph's conduct in the tranſaction now before us. Every body
knows, who knows any thing of Scripture, that the
ſpeeches made to their Children by the holy Patriarchs
of old, prior to their departure from this world, called
in the language of Scripture *Bleſſing the Children* (o),
were ſo many prophetic declarations of the Word of
God, predicting to them the future events that ſhould
diſtinguiſh them and their families, and entailing upon
them and their poſterity that portion of happineſs or
miſery, to which their moral or immoral conduct entitled them. This being an undoubted truth, let us
now examine with an attentive eye ſome of the moſt
material circumſtances of that ſolemn Bleſſing, which
Jacob beſtowed on Joſeph and his Brethren a little
before his death (p).

1. This Bleſſing was beſtowed on Joſeph and his
Brethren about four or five years after Joſeph had
enſlaved all the inhabitants of Egypt, excepting thoſe
of the Sacerdotal Order (q).

2. Jacob in this Bleſſing reproaches Reuben, his
eldeſt ſon, with the infamy of his inceſtuous crime in
the ſtrongeſt terms; and declares, that, in puniſhment
of it, *he ſhould not excel*, but ſhould be as *unſtable as
water*.

3. Simeon and Levi are branded by the holy Patriarch with being *Inſtruments of cruelty*; he abhors
their counſels; calls their company diſhonourable;
curſes

(o) Gen. 27. v. 4, 7, 10, 12, 19, &c. (p) Gen. 49, v. 1, &c.
(q) Gen. 47. 28.

curfes the fiercenefs of their anger, and the cruelty of their wrath, *becaufe in their anger*, fays he, *they flew a man*; meaning Shechem the Hivite and his father Hamor, together with all his male fubjects, whom *they flew with the fword* (r); and, as a punifhment of their barbarous cruelty, he declares they fhould be divided and fcattered in the land of Promife.

4. When the Holy Patriarch comes to blefs his fon Jofeph, he expreffes himfelf in the following emphatic and divine ftrain. "Jofeph is a fruitful bough; even "a fruitful bough by a well, whofe branches run "over the wall. The archers have forely grieved him, "and fhot at him, and hated him: but his bow abode "in ftrength, and the arms of his hands were made "ftrong by the hands of the mighty God of Jacob: "from thence is the Shepherd, the ftone of Ifrael; "even by the God of thy father, who fhall help thee, "and by the Almighty, who fhall blefs thee with blef- "fings of heaven above, bleffings of the deep that "lieth under, bleffings of the breaft, and of the womb. "The bleffings of thy father have prevailed above "the bleffings of my progenitors: unto the utmoft "bounds of the everlafting hills, they fhall be on the "head of Jofeph, and on the crown of the head of "him, that was feparate from his brethren"(s).

In thefe prophetic and beautiful expreffions, exhibiting in the moft pleafing colours the perfonal character of Jofeph, and the bleffings entailed on his pofterity, literally fulfilled afterwards, we can perceive nothing but what neceffarily fuppofes in Jofeph the greateft innocence of heart, the moft unimpeachable rectitude of conduct, and the moft gracious acceptance with his Creator. No part of his conduct is here branded

(r) Gen. 34. v. 25, 26. (s) Gen. 49. v. 22—27.

branded with difgrace, with the leaft appearance of the fmalleft guilt, or with the moft diftant intimation of reproof.

But, were the Slave-Trade as criminal in its nature as it is pretended, were it a purfuit hateful in the fight of God, and an atrocious encroachment on the facred rights of juftice and humanity, would Jacob, or, rather, would God, who fpoke by his mouth, have overlooked the atrocity of a crime big with fuch an accumulation of guilt? Would he have engaged his word to be his help and protection, and to beftow fuch a plenitude of bleffings on the crown of his head, as foon almoft as he had concluded that Slave-contract we are fpeaking of, and at the very time he was keeping in bondage fo many millions of his fellow-creatures? Would God, I fay, or could God, without a moft glaring oppofition to the effential rights of his own juftice, have acted thus in the cafe of Jofeph, and at the fame time rebuke his brethren Reuben, Simeon, and Levi in the fevereft terms, and inflict a lafting punifhment on them and their pofterity (though the former had only one accufation againft him, and the two latter pleaded in juftification of their violent proceedings the revenge due to their fifter Dinah, and the honour of their Father's houfe (*t*)), had not Jofeph's recent conduct in reducing fo many millions of free Africans to the abject condition of Slaves, as well as every other tranfaction of his life, been perfectly agreeable to the invariable tenour of thofe facred Laws, of which he alone was the Author and Judge?

To every one of thefe queftions there is but one direct anfwer; which, as it muft neceffarily be in the negative, muft of confequence evince to the meaneft

capacity

(*t*) Gen. 34. v. 7, 30, 31.

capacity, that the SLAVE-TRADE has the indifputable fanction of God in its fupport.

XXIV. I WILL not conceal, or even difguife, in favour of the Caufe I have efpoufed, what, I apprehend, will be objected to the argument I have juft enforced, from the Scriptural account of Jofeph's extenfive purchafe of African Slaves.—It will be objected, I prefume, that Jofeph's purchafe was not a forcible purchafe; that the Egyptians, whom he bought, offered themfelves of their own accord, and defired he would buy them at a certain price (v); and that, of courfe, the free and voluntary ceffion they made of their liberties and perfons juftified Jofeph's conduct, and rendered his contract juft and valid, without injuring the natural rights of juftice and humanity; which being far otherwife in the ufual practice of the SLAVE-TRADE, in which perfons are fold and bought without their confent, the inferences drawn in vindication of that Trade from the practice of Jofeph, can have no weight of conviction in fupport of the SLAVE-TRADE.—No one, I truft, will tax me with partiality to my Caufe from the ftatement of this argument againft myfelf: I have given it, I think, all the weight it is able to carry: how much it will weigh in the fcale of found and unprejudiced reafon, will foon appear from the following confiderations.

XXV. 1. I can by no means allow, that Jofeph's purchafe of Pharaoh's fubjects was not a forcible purchafe in fact, and in ftrictnefs of language. It is true, the Egyptians themfelves, without any apparent explicit propofal on the part of Jofeph, defired him to buy them for bread: but did they ever think of making that offer, whilft they had any bread to eat, or any

E   means

means left for buying or procuring it? Did not Joseph himself, prior to that offer, pave, as it were, the way to it, by engroffing all the corn in the land of Egypt, and by felling it to them for money and cattle, till they had neither money nor cattle to give in exchange? — Let us hear how they addrefs themfelves to him: their petition will beft explain, how far their offer may be called voluntary on their part. " They came un-
" to him the fecond year, *fays the facred Writer*, and
" faid unto him: We will not hide it from my Lord,
" how that our money is fpent; my Lord alfo hath
" our herds of cattle: there is not aught left in the
" fight of my Lord, but our bodies and our lands.
" *Wherefore fhall we die* before thine eyes, both we
" and our land? Buy us and our land for bread, and
" we and our land will be fervants unto Pharaoh; and
" give us feed, that *we may live and not die*, that the
" land be not defolate."
Is this the language of perfons, who freely, volun-
tarily, of their own accord, and without any compul-
fion whatever, offer themfelves to fale? Is it not evident from the very words of their own addrefs, that,
finding themfelves reduced to the laft extremity of indigence, and feeing nothing before their eyes but in-
evitable death or flavery, they were forced, through
dread of the former, to fubmit to the latter? And
can there be a more forcible contract, than that which
is made only through fear of death, only to avoid in-
evitable death? — The ceffion then made by the
Egyptians of their liberties and perfons, was neither
in fact, nor in ftrictnefs of language, nor, indeed, in
conformity with the Scriptural account of the circumftances attending it, a free and voluntary ceffion. Had
not therefore Jofeph had better grounds in the principles of his Natural Religion, of which he was a moft

ftrict

ſtrict obſerver, to aſſure himſelf of the juſtice of his contract, the ceſſion of the Egyptians, forcible in the ſtricteſt propriety of the word, would never have rendered his Contract juſt and valid in the ſight of God.

2. But even granting, for a moment, that the Egyptians did really make a free and voluntary ceſſion of their liberties and perſons; I do not ſee, upon what principle of reaſon their ceſſion could juſtify Joſeph's conduct and make his purchaſe lawful, if, as it is ſo confidently aſſerted, the SLAVE-TRADE be eſſentially unjuſt and illicit in its own nature. For, if to purchaſe thoſe of our own ſpecies be highly criminal in itſelf, be an unjuſt invaſion on the rights of juſtice and humanity, and directly oppoſite to the Sacred Laws of Nature, how is it poſſible to conceive, that any ceſſion whatever of the party to be purchaſed ſhould make that juſt and lawful in the ſight of God, which by his unalterable eternal laws is eſſentially the very reverſe? Can human agreements diſpenſe in the laws of God? Whatever is eſſentially unjuſt and illicit to purchaſe, muſt be as eſſentially unjuſt and illicit to ſale.— The objection then grounded on the pretended voluntary ceſſion of the Egyptians, however plauſible it may appear at firſt, is utterly inconcluſive and ill founded.

XXVI. I could eaſily produce a greater number of diſtinguiſhed Characters within this period of the Law of Nature, whoſe uniform manner of acting, with reference to the preſent ſubject, would afford me an additional number of arguments in vindication of the SLAVE-TRADE. But as the Sacred Book, where thoſe great Patterns of every religious and ſocial virtue are exhibited, is in every body's hands, and, as I have ſufficiently demonſtrated, I think, from the Scriptural

account

account of two of the moſt eminent Characters within the ſame period, that the SLAVE-TRADE has the indiſputable ſanction of Divine Authority, and is in exact conformity with the principles of the Law of Nature, as delineated in the Sacred Writings of the Word
of God, I ſhall now proceed to demonſtrate in the
ſubſequent Section, that it is equally conformable to
the principles of the Moſaic Law.

SECTION

SECTION II.

Scriptural Refearches on the licitnefs of the Slave-Trade, fhewing its conformity with the principles of the Mofaic Law delineated in the Sacred Writings.

I. THE Mofaic Law, called alfo the Written Law, and the Mofaic Difpenfation, fucceeded the Difpenfation of the Law of Nature : not, as if, by the publication of the former (*a*), the latter had been totally abrogated, or fuffered the leaft relaxation in any of its laws, which are of perpetual obligation ; but becaufe the Almighty willing to eftablifh a Covenant with his Chofen People, the Children of Ifrael, added to the former obligations fuch other ftatutes, Laws, and ceremonies, as were to diftinguifh them from every other Nation in the World. This Law is very frequently called, even in Scripture, the Law of Mofes (*b*), and Mofes is faid to have been the Lawgiver or the Legiflator of the Children of Ifrael ; not becaufe it was framed by him, but becaufe the Almighty delivered it to them through his miniftry, and he committed it to writing. How long this Law was in force from the firft promulgation of it, has been the fubjeét of much inquiry among the Learned : but, without entering now into a critical difcuffion of this controverted point, we may fafely venture to fix that period, without either advantage or prejudice to the Subjeét of our Refearches, to the time of the Apoftles Council held at Jerufalem, in which the Law of Circumcifion and other Legal obfervances were, by an exprefs

(*a*) Exod. c. 29, &c.
(*b*) Jofh. c. 8. v. 31, 32. Ibid. 23. 6. I. Kings, 2. 3. II. Kings, 23, 25.

exprefs Decree of that Council, declared unneceffary to Salvation, and confequently of no further obligation (*c*). This Council, according to the computation of Archbifhop Ufher, was held in the Year of the World 4055; and as the Law was promulged in the Year 2513, according to the chronological computation of the fame Author; it follows, that the Law of Mofes, or the Mofaic Difpenfation, continued in force 1542 Years.

II. Now, before I proceed to fhew, that the Laws and principles of this fecond Divine Difpenfation of Religion, not only never prohibited the Slave-Trade, but gave, on the contrary, a pofitive fanction to the profecution of it; I judge neceffary to apprize the Reader, that the arguments I mean to enforce in vindication of the Slave-Trade, as confined to this fecond period of true Religion, fhall be entirely grounded on fuch written laws and principles of internal moral rectitude, as conftituted the true morality of that Religion; and not on fuch Legal obfervances and practices, as were peculiar to it, and conftituted only the ritual, typical, or ceremonial part of its frame. The following decifive inftances of the former fort, will, without producing others, be fufficient, I hope, to eftablifh my affertion beyond the power of reply.

E X O D U S.

III. It is fingular enough, that the very firft Law, or *Judgement*, in the Scripture language, enacted by God himfelf immediately after he had delivered the Ten Commandments to his People, fhould be refpecting the Slave-Trade; and that alfo with the additional circumftance of not reftraining them from purchafing their own brethren, their own flefh and blood!

"Thefe

(*c*) Acts; 15, 1, &c.

" These are the judgements, *says God to Moses*, which
" thou fhalt fet before them. If thou buy an Hebrew
" Servant, fix years he fhall ferve, and in the feventh
" he fhall go out free for nothing. If he came in by
" himfelf, he fhall go out by himfelf; if he were
" married, then his wife fhall go out with him. If
" his Mafter have given him a wife, and fhe have
" borne him fons and daughters; the wife and her
" children fhall be her Mafter's, and he fhall go out
" by himfelf. (*d*)"

IV. Here, it is evident in the firft place, that, however limited the time was of the Slavery of an Hebrew, he was yet in the ftrickeft fenfe of the word a
true and real Slave for the time; for he was his Mafter's property, bought for a certain price; and his
Mafter, on this account, had an undoubted right and
power to fell him again to another perfon before the
expiration of that time. But, were the SLAVE-TRADE,
or the purchafing of thofe of our own fpecies, and
dealing in human flefh, a purfuit of that heinous and
crying nature, as to be effentially unlawful, effentially
incompatible with the principles of reafon, nature, and
true Religion, would God, Juftice and Sanctity itfelf,
have authorized the practice of it with fo pofitive, fo
manifeft, fo explicit a fanction, I do not fay for the
fpace of fix years, but even for a fingle moment, at
the very time he was making his Holy Covenant with
his chofen People, and teaching them the very principles of true Religion?

Again: the Hebrew, thus bought by his Brother,
and reduced to the condition of a Slave, under the
exprefs fanction of God, was a Child of the Circumcifion: now, Circumcifion, under the Mofaic Difpenfation, was a folemn, religious Rite anfwering that of
Baptifm

(*d*) Exod. c. 21. v. 1—4.

Baptifm in the Chriftian Law : it was a token of the Covenant between God and his People (*e*), as effentially requifite in every male perfon, who hoped for acceptance with God (*f*), as is Baptifm in the Covenant of the New Law. If then, notwithftanding the prerogative of Circumcifion, which made the profeffors of the Mofaic Law true Children of God, true believers, and members of his Church, a free circumcifed Ifraelite was ftill fubject to the law of human bondage or flavery, and that even under the dominion of one of his own Communion and Church ; from what maxim or principle of true Religion and juftice does it follow, that a Slave, once admitted into the Covenant of the New Law, acquires by his admiffion a right to his emancipation from human bondage ? that is, a right to deprive his Mafter of his property ?

In fine ; it is manifeft from the very letter of the Law juft quoted, that, even in the Cafe of an Hebrew reduced to the condition of a Slave for a limited time, the Mafter's purchafe of that Slave was fo effentially juft and lawful in every part of it, that, though, by an efpecial ordinance of God peculiar to that People only, the Slave was to be releafed from bondage in the feventh year, or the year of the Jubilee ; yet the right of property, acquired by that purchafe, was declared by God to be fo vefted in the Mafter, that, if the Mafter had given a wife to his Slave, that is, if the Slave had married a wife during the time of his fervitude with the confent of his Mafter, both fhe and her children, if he had any by her, became the Mafter's property for ever : in which Cafe, it is worth obferving, that the Slave thus emancipated, though a member of the true Church, was ordered to *go out by himfelf*, and leave his wife and children behind.—A feparation

ration

(*e*) Gen. c. 17. v. 11.   (*f*) Gen. 17. 14.

ration this between hufband and wife, father and children, well deferving the particular attention of every religious and humane advocate for African Liberty !— And can any one after this entertain the moft diftant doubt on the licitnefs of the Slave-Trade, fo pofitively, fo unequivocally, fo ftrongly authorized by this written ordinance of the Word of God?

LEVITICUS.

V. The farther I proceed in my Scriptural Refearches, the ftronger the evidences appear to me in favour of the Slave-Trade. Indeed, I have every encouragement given me in this Sacred Book of Leviticus to advance a ftep farther, and maintain, that the Slave-Trade, has not only the fanction of Divine Authority in its fupport, but was alfo pofitively encouraged (I had almoft faid, *commanded*) by that Authority, under the Difpenfation of the Mofaic Law. The following plain and explicit words of one of the laws refpecting that Trade, and regiftered in this Book, can admit of no other conftruction.

" Both thy bond-men and bond-maids, *fays the Su-*
" *preme Law-giver,* which thou fhalt have, fhall be
" of the heathen that are round about you ; of them
" fhall ye buy bond-men and bond-maids. More-
" over, of the Children of the Strangers that do fo-
" journ among you ; of them fhall ye buy ; and of
" their families that are with you, which they begat
" in your land : and they fhall be your poffeffion.
" And ye fhall take them as an inheritance for your
" children after you to inherit them for a poffeffion ;
" they fhall be your bond-men for ever" (g).

VI. If there be meaning in language, or fenfe in words, here is certainly a Law enacted by Divine Authority, which does not only give a moft pofitive and

F   unexceptionable

(g) Leviticus, c. 25. v. 44—46.

unexceptionable fanction to the licitnefs of the SLAVE-
· TRADE, but feems farther to lay, as it were, an injunc-
tion on the Children of Ifrael to profecute that Traf-
fic under no other reftriction whatever, but that of
confining their purchafes of perpetual Slaves to the
heathen round about them, and the Strangers, that
fojourned among ; for the words of the Law-giver
evidently imply more than a mere permiffion or leave :
He does not fay, fpeaking of the Heathen and Sojourners, *Of them* MAY *ye buy bond-men and bond-maids*,
but, *of them* SHALL *ye buy bond-men and bond-maids.*

AGAIN : the words of this Law, and they are the
words of God, do exprefsly declare, that Slaves thus
purchafed from the Heathen and Sojourners among
them, fhall be the *Poffeffion*, that is, the real and lawful property, of the purchafers : a property fo ftrict-
ly their own, that they fhall bequeath it to their Children at their death, as a part of their juft and lawful
inheritance, a part of their paternal eftate, an eftate
for ever, for *they fhall be your bond-men for ever*, fays
the Law : that is, an hereditary eftate with all the
emoluments arifing from it ; and, confequently, with
all the children born from them, agreeably to the tenour of that Law of EXODUS, which has been explain-
ed in the IV th Number of this SECTION ; for otherwife the children of a Heathen Slave or a Stranger
would have enjoyed a privilege, which an Hebrew
Slave was denied, though a Slave only for a limited
time.

VII. FROM this moft decifive, moft explicit, and .
irrefragable authority of the Written Word of God,
vifibly encouraging the profecution of the SLAVE-
TRADE, and declaring in the moft categorical language that words can devife, that a Slave is the real,
indifputable, and lawful property of the purchafer and
his heirs for ever, it neceffarily follows by force of
consequence,

consequence, that either the SLAVE-TRADE must be in
its own intrinsic nature a just and an honest Trade, and
by no means deserving those harsh epithets and names
with which it is so frequently branded and degraded;
or, that, if it does still deserve those odious names and
epithets in consequence of its intrinsic turpitude and
immorality, the Almighty did so far forget himself,
when he made the above Law, as to patronize a manifest injustice, encourage a most criminal violation of
his other laws, and give his sacred sanction to what
humanity itself must for ever abhor and detest.—As
there can be no medium betwixt these two unavoidable
inferences, and the latter is one of the most daring
blasphemies that the human heart can conceive, I leave
the religious Reader to judge for himself, which side
of the Question is the safest to embrace.

J O S H U A.

VIII. THE prudent and well concerted stratagem of
the inhabitants of Gibeon, with all the circumstances
attending its final issue, so minutely described in the
IX th Chapter of this Sacred Book, will, when viewed
in its proper light, add no small weight of authority to
the justice of the SLAVE-TRADE. The Scriptural account of this entertaining transaction, long as it may
appear to some, cannot well be contracted, without
injuring its beautiful texture: the following is a literal
transcript of it.

v. 3. And when the inhabitants of Gibeon heard what
Joshua had done unto Jericho, and to Ai,

4. They did work wilily, and went and made as if
they had been Ambassadors, and took old sacks upon their asses, and wine-bottles, old, and rent and
bound up:

5. And old shoes, and clouted upon their feet, and old
garments upon them: and all the bread of their
provision was dry and mouldy.

6. And

6. And they went to Joſhua, unto the Camp of Gilgal, and ſaid unto him, and to the men of Iſrael : we be come from a far country; now therefore make ye a league with us.

7. And the men of Iſrael ſaid unto the Hivites : peradventure ye dwell among us, and how ſhall we make a league with you ?

8. And they ſaid unto Joſhua: we are thy ſervants. And Joſhua ſaid unto them : who are ye ? and from whence come ye ?

9. And they ſaid unto him : from a very far country thy ſervants are come, becauſe of the name of the Lord thy God; for we have heard of the fame of him, and all that he did in Egypt,

10. And all that he did to the two Kings of the Amorites, that were beyond Jordan, to Sihon King of Heſhbon, and to Og King of Baſhan, which was at Aſhtaroth.

11. Wherefore our Elders and all the Inhabitants of our country ſpake to us, ſaying : take victuals with you for the journey, and go to meet them, and ſay unto them: we are your ſervants : therefore now make ye a league with us.

12. This our bread we took hot for our proviſion out of our houſes, on the day we came forth to go unto you; but now behold, it is dry, and it is mouldy. :

13. And theſe bottles of wine which were filled, were new ; and behold, they be rent; and theſe our garments and our ſhoes are become old, by reaſon of the very long journey.

14. And the men took of their victuals, and aſked not counſel at the mouth of the Lord.

15. And Joſhua made peace with them, and made a league with them, to let them live : and the Princes of the Congregation ſware unto them.

16. And

16. And it came to pass at the end of three days, after they had made a league with them, that they heard that they were neighbours, and that they dwelt among them.

17. And the Children of Israel journeyed, and came into their Cities on the third day: now their Cities were Gibeon, and Chephirah, and Beeroth, and Kiriath-jearim.

18. And the Children of Israel smote them not, because the Princes of the Congregation had sworn unto them by the Lord God of Israel: and all the Congregation murmured against the Princes.

19. But all the Princes said unto all the Congregation: We have sworn unto them by the Lord God of Israel: now therefore we may not touch them.

20. This we will do them; we will even let them live, lest wrath be upon us, because of the oath which we sware unto them.

21. And the Princes said unto them: let them live (but let them be hewers of wood, and drawers of water unto all the Congregation), as the Princes had promised them.

22. And Joshua called for them, and he spake unto them, saying: wherefore have ye beguiled us, saying, We are very far from you? when ye dwell among us.

23. Now therefore ye are cursed, and there shall none of you be freed from being bond-men, and hewers of wood, and drawers of water for the house of my God.

24. And they answered Joshua, and said: because it was certainly told thy servants, how that the Lord thy God commanded his servant Moses to give you all the land, and to destroy all the inhabitants of the land from before you, therefore we were sore afraid
of

of our lives, becaufe of you, and have done this
thing.

25. And now, behold, we are in thine hand: as it
feemeth good and right unto thee to do unto us, do.

26. And fo did he unto them, and delivered them out
of the hand of the Children of Ifrael, and they flew
them not.

27. And Jofhua made them that day hewers of wood,
and drawers of water for the Congregation, and for
the Altar of the Lord, even unto this day, in the
place which he fhould chufe.

IX. The following obfervations feem to arife fpon-
taneoufly from the circumftances related in this interefting portion of Scripture.

1. The Gibeonites were in the number of thofe inhabitants of the Land of Canaan, who, by the exprefs
command of God, were to be utterly profcribed, and
driven out of the Land, by the Children of Ifrael:
*Thou fhalt make no covenant with them, nor with their
Gods*, faid the Almighty to his People; *they fhall not
dwell in thy Land* (h).

2. To ward this impending doom, of which they
were well apprized, as appears from their reply to
Jofhua, they had recourfe to a ftratagem, which, for
want of Jofhua confulting the divine Oracle, fucceeded
to the utmoft of their wifhes; for they made a league,
and a treaty of peace and amity with Jofhua and his
People; and by virtue of this National Treaty, which
was confirmed to them with the folemn fanction of an
oath, and never annulled, but rather ratified in the
fequel by God himfelf, they were exempted from the
general doom, and became in every fenfe of the word
free allies and friends to the Children of Ifrael.—Indeed, the fentiments of Religion and humility, fo
vifible

(h) Exod, c. 23. v. 31—33.

vifible both in their firft addrefs and their reply to Jofhua's charge, and their not joining in the general league of the neighbouring Kings, who all combined *with one accord* to fight againft Ifrael (*i*), fpeak a fenfe of repentance, which might have induced the Almighty to reverfe his fentence, and fuffer their ftratagem to fucceed.

3. As foon as this was difcovered, we find, that the Gibeonites were all configned by Jofhua to perpetual Slavery, *unto this day*; that is, with all their pofterity; notwithftanding the fentence of profcription, the only one that the Almighty had pronounced againft them, and was to be executed by Jofhua, had been entirely reverfed; notwithftanding they had every claim, by virtue of the recent Treaty they had fo folemnly concluded with him and his People, to all the privileges and franchifes of free Allies.

X. To fay, that the fentence of death pronounced againft the Gibeonites in feveral places of Scripture (*k*), was afterwards changed by the Almighty into that of perpetual and hereditary bondage or flavery, is to advance what is never to be found in any part of the Sacred Records; from the wole tenour of which it appears manifeft, that the perpetual bondage, to which they were configned with all their pofterity, was the fole act and deed of Jofhua, fuggefted apparently by the Princes of the Congregation of Ifrael, who, prior to Jofhua's curfe upon them, in order to filence the murmurs of the multitude, had declared their intention of employing the Gibeonites in the fervile occupation of *hewers of wood, and drawers of water unto all the Congregation.*

Now, had Jofhua's fentence of perpetual bondage been only a commutation of that of death, to which the

(*i*) Jofh. c. 9. v. 1, 2. (*k*) Exod. 23. 31—33. Deut. 7. 2. &c.

the Almighty had condemned the Gibeonites, had it not been lawful in itself, on other accounts, to reduce the innocent as well as the guilty to the condition of Slaves; the sentence of perpetual bondage pronounced by Joshua, ought, one would imagine, to have extended no farther, than the persons of the Gibeonites then living, any more than did the sentence of death, in lieu of which that of perpetual bondage is said to have been substituted. The slavery then of their innocent posterity, at least, cannot be said to have been in lieu of death, to which certainly they had never been condemned.

It being therefore evident from the uniform tenour of the Sacred Writings, that neither the reduction of the Gibeonites then living, nor that of their guiltless descendants, yet unborn, to perpetual Slavery, was ever condemned by any mark or intimation whatever of God's displeasure, but manifestly ratified in the sequel by several undoubted assurances of his divine approbation; it is easy to conclude, whether the reducing of the innocent as well as the guilty part of our fellow-creatures to the condition of Slaves, or even to hereditary bondage or Slavery, be in its own nature licit or illicit, criminal or unjust.

XI. As a mark of the Almighty's undoubted approbation of Joshua's conduct in the transaction just before us, we find in the continuation of this history (l), that He even secured to his People the possession of these Slaves, and their posterity, by a most signal victory, which he enabled them to obtain over five Kings of the Amorites; who, in consequence of the Gibeonites having made a league and a treaty of peace with Joshua and his People, joined all their forces against them, and made a vigorous attempt to invade
this

(l) Josh. c. 10.

this new acquisition of the Children of Israel. The exertions of his divine power for securing to his People this new acquired property of Slaves were so wonderfully great, that he even fought *in Person* against the invaders; for " The Lord, *says the Sacred Writer*, " discomfitted them before Israel, and flew them with " a great slaughter at Gibeon, and chased them along " the way that goeth up to Bethhoron, and smote them " to Azekah, and unto Makkedah. And it came to " pass, as they fled from before Israel, and were in " the going down to Bethhoron, that the Lord cast " down great stones from heaven upon them unto " Azekah, and they died: they were more which died " with hailstones, than they whom the Children of " Israel flew with the sword" (*m*).

AND, in order to render the victory still more complete, and the part he took in defending the rights of his People over the Gibeonites more visible to the whole world, he even wrought a miracle of the most singular kind; for, *harkning*, as the Sacred Page expresses it, *unto the voice of a Man*, that is, of Joshua, who, in the heat of action, ordered *the Sun to stand still upon Gibeon, and the Moon in the valley of Ajalon,* he stayed them both *about a whole day, until the People had avenged themselves upon their enemies* (*n*), for attempting to destroy the inhabitants of Gibeon their bond-slaves.

XII. IF these wonderful atchievements of the power of God in favour of his chosen People in the very case of protecting the persons, whom they had so lately reduced to perpetual and hereditary bondage, are not to be considered as so many evident testimonies of his divine approbation of the immediate object of the SLAVE-TRADE, and a positive sanction to the licitness

G of

(*m*) Josh. c. 10. v. 10, 11, (*n*) Josh. c. 10. v. 12, 14.

of it, but are still consistent with any intrinsic moral turpitude inherent to the nature of that Trade; the abettors of this opinion must necessarily maintain, that the Supreme Ruler of the Universe, in direct opposition to his own essential attributes and perfections, in manifest contradiction with his own moral laws and commandments, and in vindication of ill-gotten property, displayed to the World the most extraordinary exertions of his Omnipotence, and disturbed the very course of Nature to make it subservient to the vilest of purposes, injustice and oppression.—As the inference is as blasphemous as it is necessary, the very mentioning of it will, I flatter myself, be sufficient to determine the judgement of any religious and candid Reader in favour of the inherent moral licitness of the SLAVE-TRADE.

XIII. I HAVE, I think, sufficiently proved from the Scriptural Passages I have produced in the series of this SECOND PART, that the SLAVE-TRADE has the positive sanction of Divine Authority in its support, and is perfectly consonant to the Principles of the Mosaic Dispensation delineated in the Sacred Writings of the Word of God.

I HAVE, however, this one thing to observe before I proceed to the THIRD PART, in order to preclude every avenue to groundless objections; that there is not a Place in all the Writings of the Word of God, whether of the OLD or of the NEW TESTAMENT, that does so much as insinuate in the most distant manner, that the Slaves bought either within the period of the Law of Nature, that of the Mosaic Dispensation, or that of the Christian Law, were to serve during a certain number of years and no longer, except the Hebrew Slaves; who, for reasons peculiar only to that People, and not applicable even to Christian Slaves, were to

ferve

ferve no longer than fix years in the capacity of Bond-Slaves. In every other cafe, the words BOND-MAN, BOND-WOMAN, BOND-MAID, BOND-SERVANT, SERVANT UNDER THE YOKE, imply, in the Scripture-language, perpetual and unlimited bondage, bondage for life, both of the male and female reduced to that condition, and even of their pofterity or children, if they had any.—Nor is there one inftance to be met with in the Sacred Volumes, of the manumiffion or emancipation of a Slave of either fex, except of the Hebrew race, who ever obtained releafe from bondage, on account of having ferved any determinate number of years.

THE difmiffion of Hagar, bond-woman to Abraham, from her Mafter's houfe, is fo far from being an inftance of this kind, that every circumftance attending her difcharge feems to prove the very reverfe (o). She was *fent away* by Abraham, at the earneft folicitation of his wife Sarai, whofe counfel the Almighty ordered him to follow : but the reluctance he fhewed to turn her out of his houfe, when it was firft propofed to him by Sarai, for *the thing was very grievous in his fight* (or, according to the Original, *The word was very bad in the eyes of Abraham*), and the reafon of her difmiffion, evidently fhew that her difcharge was not in confequence of any contract whatever, by which fhe was bound to ferve a determinate number of years and no longer, there being not the leaft intimation given in the Sacred Hiftory of any fuch contract or agreement, but becaufe her fon's behaviour to Ifaac, the promifed and right Heir of the Family, was exceedingly odious and very alarming to Sarai ; who, dreading the confequences of Ifhmael's *perfecution* of young Ifaac, for fo the Apoftle ftyles it (*p*), infifted on his being *caft out* together with his mother Hagar.

G 2

XIV. THE

(o) Gen. 21. v. 9—14. (p) Galat. c. 4. v. 29.

XIV. The Scriptural acceptation and extent of the word Bondage, and the relatives to it, being thus fixed and afcertained from the very letter and uniform tenour of Scripture itfelf, no arguments whatever, grounded on the true and real fenfe in which that word and its relatives are ufed in the Sacred Page, will ever evince, that a Slave, within the period of any of the Three Difpenfations of true Religion mentioned in the Sacred Annals of the Word of God, not born an Hebrew, was ever bound by contract or otherwife to ferve only a limited number of years, at the expiration of which he obtained his freedom, and was left at liberty to chufe for himfelf.

SECTION

SECTION III.

Scriptural Researches on the licitness of the Slave-Trade, shewing its conformity with the principles of the Christian Dispensation delineated in the Sacred Writings.

I. THE Christian Dispensation, called frequently the Christian Law, the Law of Christ, the Christian Religion, the Law of Grace, the New Law, and the New Covenant or the New Testament, is that most sublime and perfect System of Faith and morality, which the Eternal Wisdom of the Father, Christ Jesus our Lord, both preached in Person, and sealed with his precious blood. As this New Law and Gospel of salvation is to remain in full force until the consummation of all things, or till time shall be no more, it is not in the power of any creature to ascertain the exact time of its duration and existence from the first promulgation of it; for *Of that day, and that hour knoweth no man, no not the Angels which are in heaven, neither the* SON, *but the* FATHER (*a*)

II. THE principal transactions relative to this New Law are registered in the several inspired Writings, that compose the Sacred Volume commonly styled THE NEW TESTAMENT. The principles and moral duties of perpetual obligation respecting *Right* and *Wrong, Justice* and *Injustice,* registered in this Sacred Volume, being evidently dictated by the HOLY SPIRIT of God, and God himself, cannot consistently with the essential infallibility of his eternal Wisdom, bear the least opposition to the principles and moral duties of perpetual obligation respecting, in like manner, *Right* and *Wrong, Justice* and *Injustice,* dictated by the same

(*a*) Mark, c. 13. v. 32.

fame infallible SPIRIT, and regiftered in the feveral infpired Writings, that compofe the Sacred Volume commonly ftyled THE OLD TESTAMENT, comprehending fuch tranfactions, as relate to both the Natural and the Mofaic Laws. — Were it poffible to be other-wife, God would not be confiftent with himfelf, and the Religion of the New Teftament, inftead of being the perfection and accomplifhment, would be the reproach and condemnation of both the former Laws, Natural and Mofaic, on the truth of which its very exiftence depends.

III. FROM this undeniable pofition it follows necef-farily, that, as the Writings of both the Teftaments have the fame weight of Authority, effentially inca-pable of contradicting itfelf, in fupport of thofe prin-ciples and decifions, enacted and regiftered in their refpective Records, concerning the intrinfic morality or immorality of human actions, whatever is declared in the One to be intrinfically good or bad, juft or un-juft, licit or illicit, muft inevitably be fo according to the principles of the Other. — If therefore, the SLAVE-TRADE appears, as, I truft, it does, from the preced-ing train of Scriptural arguments, in perfect harmony with the principles and decifions of the Word of God, regiftered in the Sacred Writings of the Old Tefta-ment, refpecting the intrinfic nature of that Trade, this, of courfe, can bear no oppofition to, but muft neceffarily be in equal perfect harmony with, the prin-ciples and decifions of the Word of God refpecting *Right* and *Juftice*, regiftered in the Sacred Writings of the New.

THIS general but forcible argument, were it even unfupported by any collateral evidences from the Writings of the New Teftament, would be fully fuffi-cient to verify my third and laft affertion refpecting
the

the Licitnefs of the SLAVE-TRADE, as perfectly conformable to the principles of the Chriftian Difpenfation.

IV. I HAVE been the more particular in bringing
this laft part of my Scriptural Refearches to this cen-
tral point of view, as I have more than one reafon to
apprehend, that feveral of my Readers will be apt to
imagine, that, by the eftablifhment of the Chriftian
Religion, the Law of Mofes was wholly abolifhed and
annulled in every part of it, and to every intent and
purpofe, both typical and moral, of its original inf-
titution; and that, of courfe, the arguments drawn
in vindication of the SLAVE-TRADE from the Writings of the Old Teftament, can have no weight of
conviction or authority with perfons, who are fubject
to no other Laws and Ordinances, but thofe of a Difpenfation, by which that was entirely laid afide.

V. TRUE as this affertion is with refpect to the ritual, typical, and ceremonial part of the Mofaic Law,
which, in this fenfe, is now utterly abolifhed, and no
longer obligatory to the Profeffors of the Gofpel, it
is not lefs erroneous and falfe with refpect to thofe
fundamental principles of righteoufnefs enacted in
that Law, which relate to the intrinfic morality or
immorality, licitnefs or illicitnefs of human actions;
which, from the invariable nature of *Right* and *Wrong*,
Juftice and *Injuftice*, muft be of perpetual obligation,
and as unchangeable as God himfelf; who never did,
nor ever could alter by any Difpenfation whatever
thofe eternal principles and laws, which are the very
bafis and foundation of true Religion, and confequently of the Religion of Chrift.

WE have no lefs an authority in confirmation of this
indifputable Doctrine, than the very words of the Son
of God, who, in that divine Sermon on the Mount,

in

in which he gave his Difciples a moft minute and circumftantial account of the principles and tenets of his Gofpel, condemned the above erroneous opinion in the moft explicit terms, and forbade them even to think of it: *Think not,* faid he, *that I am come to deftroy the Law or the Prophets; I am not come to deftroy but to fulfil (b).*

IT was on the principle of this Doctrine of the Son of God, and on purpofe to guard againft every exception to arguments drawn from the Writings of the Old Teftament in favour of the SLAVE-TRADE, which fome perfons would be apt to make in confequence of the above erroneous opinion, that I efpecially apprized the Reader in the II ᵈ Number of the laft SECTION, that the arguments I meant to enforce in that Section in vindication of that Trade, would be entirely grounded, as they certainly are, on fuch written and explicit laws and principles of internal moral rectitude, as conftituted the true morality of the Mofaic Difpenfation, and not on fuch Legal obfervances and practices, as were peculiar to it, and conftituted only the ritual, typical, or ceremonial part of its frame.

VI. THE permanent and indefectible authority of the Old Teftament, and the neceffary conformity of the New with the principles and declarations of the former refpecting the intrinfic nature of *Right* and *Wrong, Juftice* and *Injuftice,* being thus firmly eftablifhed and afcertained; I fhall now proceed, for argument's fake, to fubftantiate in a more particular manner the merits of the prefent Controverfy with reference to the principles and tenets of the New Teftament; which, from the unanfwerable, though general, argument juft enforced, appears already to give a fanction to the licitnefs of the SLAVE-TRADE, the intrinfic morality of which is fo evidently warranted
by

(b) Matt. c. 5. v. 17.

by thofe invariable principles and decifions of the Old, with which, as proved before, it muft neceff'rily agree.

VII. THAT there is nothing in the Writings of the New Teftament, that can be produced in juftification of the SLAVE-TRADE, has been confidently afferted by many; and from this *fuppofed filence* of the Infpired Writers, they have as confidently concluded, that the profeffors of Chriftianity are not juftifiable in profecuting a Trade, which, not having, in their opinion, the Sanction of the New Teftament, muft of courfe be effentially oppofite to the principles of true Chriftianity, which forbids in the moft explicit terms, and under the fevereft punifhments, all acts of injuftice, unnaturalnefs, and oppreffion.

VIII. The ftronger this inference, founded indeed on a falfe fuppofition, appears to the Advocates for African Liberty againft the licitnefs of the SLAVE-TRADE, the more powerful the following arguments muft appear to them; which, from the fame negative principle, not of *fuppofed*, but *real*, filence refpecting the pretended illicitnefs of it, amounting in fact to a pofitive fanction in our Cafe, feem manifeftly to evince, that the SLAVE-TRADE bears no oppofition whatever to the principles of the Chriftian Law.

1. IF the Writings of the New Teftament mention nothing, as it is *falfely fuppofed*, in vindication of the SLAVE-TRADE, neither do they *in reality* and *truth* mention any thing in condemnation of it; if then the *fuppofed* filence of the Infpired Writers refpecting the licitnefs of that Trade, that is, their not mentioning that Trade at all, as it is *fuppofed*, can be brought as an argument of its moral inconfiftency with the principles of true Chriftianity; the *real* filence of the fame refpecting the pretended illicitnefs of it, that is, their not condemning the Trade at all, though publickly

H

blickly practifed in their time, and by the very perfons whom they were deputed to teach the principles and duties of Chriftianity, muft be a ftronger argument by far of the inherent moral conformity of the SLAVE-TRADE with the principles and tenets of the Religion of Chrift : for it fhews in the ftrongeft light, that the firft Teachers of Chriftianity, who were alfo the Infpired Writers of the New Teftament, never confidered the SLAVE-TRADE, or had been taught by their Mafter to confider it, as an infraction of any of the principles or moral precepts of his Gofpel.

2, In effect; this conftant and uniform filence of the Sacred Writers of the New Teftament in a matter of fuch public notoriety; I mean their never difapproving the practice of a Trade, in which the rights of Chriftian juftice and humanity are faid to be fo materially injured, ought to attract the particular attention of every impartial inquirer into the merits of the prefent Controverfy.

IT is an abfolute fact, attefted by all Hiftorians, both Sacred and Prophane, that at the very time that Chriftianity made its appearance in the World, as well as at the time that the Apoftles and Difciples of Chrift were employed in preaching and propagating throughout the World his holy Gofpel and Doctrine, both before and after the fame had been committed to writing, that is, before and after the New Teftament was written, that the practice of Slavery, or the SLAVE-TRADE, was univerfally adopted by the very Nations to whom they brought the glad tidings of falvation, and who, through faith, repentance, and obedience to the maxims and doctrine they preached, were received into the Covenant of reconciliation and grace; and yet it is not lefs certain from the conftant tenour of the Sacred Writings of the New Teftament, that defifting from the profecution of the SLAVE-TRADE, or manumitting thofe who were in actual bondage, was never declared by any of the Apoftles

tles or firft Teachers of Chriftianity to be a neceffary term of Salvation or acceptance with God, or an indifpenfable duty of a follower of Chrift.

But were the Trade fo diametrically oppofite to the principles of Chriftianity, as it is afferted, were it a moft unjuftifiable ufurpation of the facred rights of juftice and humanity, would the Apoftles have fuffered thofe facred rights to be thus invaded and trampled upon with impunity, without fo much as fignifying to thofe, whom they were commiffioned to teach the Gofpel of righteoufnefs and peace, of love and charity; that it was in open contradiction with the principles and precepts of that Gofpel?

3. In fine: this manner of reafoning to prove the moral conformity of the Slave-Trade with the principles of the Chriftian Difpenfation, acquires a degree of irrefiftible force, when applied to the conduct of our Bleffed Saviour in his public character of Founder and Teacher of the New Law; for though he embraced every opportunity of reproving in the fevereft terms fuch irreligious abufes as were practifed by the Jews, and of rectifying fuch falfe gloffes, traditions, and comments, as had been added by them to the Law of Mofes; yet he never once condemned, reproved, or even hinted the leaft difapprobation of the practice of Slavery, fo generally adopted in his time : no, not even in his Divine Sermon on the Mount, in which he fpoke on fet purpofe of the moft exalted duties of his Religion, entered into a minute and moft circumftantial detail of many reciprocal offices and duties he required of his followers, and rectified fome abufes, incomparably lefs criminal than would be that of enflaving our fellow creatures, were this practice fo very criminal and unjuft as is reprefented by fome modern advocates for African Liberty (c).

H 2

4. The

(c) Matt. cc. 5. 6. 7.

4. THE fact is: that, fince neither the SON of God, being himfelf God, nor his Difciples commiffioned to teach his doctrine, could ever alter the intrinfic nature of *Right* and *Wrong*; once the practice of Slavery, or the SLAVE-TRADE, had been exprefsly declared by the FATHER effentially juft and lawful in the Sacred Writings of the Old Law, which the SON *did not come to deftroy, but to fulfil* (*d*), it was abfolutely impoffible, that either HE or his Difciples fhould declare it unlawful and unjuft in the Writings of the New, the principles of both the Laws, refpecting the intrinfic nature of *Right* and *Wrong*, *Juftice* and *Injuftice*, being invariably the fame.

IT follows then, that the argument drawn in favour of the SLAVE-TRADE from the conftant filence of the Infpired Writers of the New Teftament refpecting the pretended illicitnefs of that Trade, that is, from their never mentioning any thing againft the licitnefs of it, which, in the circumftances above related, would have been only a negative inference, though of confiderable weight in vindication of it, becomes now, from this laft very material circumftance, a moft powerful pofitive argument, fhewing in the ftrongeft light, that the nature of the SLAVE-TRADE is perfectly confonant to the principles and tenets of the Chriftian Law.

IX. THOUGH the argument built on the *fuppofed filence* of the Infpired Writers of the New Teftament refpecting the licitnefs of the SLAVE-TRADE, is very amply confuted by the preceding arguments drawn from the *real filence* of the fame Sacred Writers refpecting the pretended illicitnefs of it, which are, indeed, abundantly fufficient to eftablifh beyond the power of cavil or reply this laft part of my SCRIPTURAL RESEARCHES; yet, left any one fhould ftill perfift in
maintaining

(*d*) Matt, c. 5. v. 17.

maintaining the opinion fo generally received, that there is nothing *pofitive* in the Writings of the New Teftament, that can be produced in juftification of the Slave-Trade, I think it expedient to felect one or two principal inftances out of thefe Sacred Books, which, I flatter myfelf, will not only gratify his curiofity, but ferve to convince him in the plaineft manner, that, however general his opinion may be, it is not fo evident as he has been taught to believe.

I. EPISTLE TO TIMOTHY.

X. Among the feveral inftructions given in this Epistle by St. Paul to his beloved Difciple Timothy for the Government of the Church of Ephefus, of which he was Bifhop, there are fome concerning the general duties of that part of his Flock, who were under the yoke of bondage or Slavery, that feem to claim our particular attention. The inftructions, here alluded to, are in the VIᵗʰ Chapter of this Epistle, and are the following : —

v. 1. Let as many fervants as are under the yoke, count their own Mafters worthy of all honour, that the name of God, and his doctrine, be not blafphemed.

2. And they that have believing Mafters, let them not defpife them, becaufe they are brethren : but rather do them fervice, becaufe they are faithful and beloved, partakers of the benefit. Thefe things teach and exhort.

3. If any man teach otherwife, and confent not to wholefome words, even the words of our Lord Jefus Chrift, and to the doctrine which is according to godlinefs,

4. He is proud, knowing nothing, but doting about queftions, and ftrifes of words, whereof cometh envy, ftrife, railings, evil furmifings, &c.

XI. The

XI. THE Apoftle in thefe words defcribes two claffes of Chriftian Slaves, or Servants under the yoke of bondage: Slaves fubject to unbelievers, and Slaves fubject to true believers or Chriftians; and, according to their refpective fituations, he fpecifies the general duties belonging to each clafs.

1. THE former are exhorted to *count their own Maf-ters*, though Infidels, *worthy of all honour*: that is, they are exhorted to fhew their Mafters, both in words and actions, fuch unfeigned marks of honour, fub-miffion, and refpect, as they have a right to claim, for *they are worthy of all honour*, from the fuperiority of their rank and ftation in life, and the authority they have acquired over them by the poffeffion of their perfons. The reafon for enforcing fuch dutiful de-portment is very powerful: you are to exhort them, fays the Apoftle to Timothy, to behave in this beco-ming manner, *that the name of God, and his doctrine, be not blafphemed*: that is, left the unbelieving Maf-ters, feeing the contrary deportment in their Chriftian Slaves, attribute their infolent, difrefpectful, and dif-obedient conduct, to the principles and doctrine of their Religion, and thus bring reproach and infamy upon both.

2. THE latter Clafs of Chriftian Slaves, fubject to Chriftian Mafters, are earneftly exhorted, not only not to be lefs refpectful and obfequious to the latter for being their brethren in Chrift, and joint-members with them of the fame Communion and Church, as if they were their equals in every refpect, but to fhow, on this very account, in their readinefs and zeal to ferve them, a fuperior degree of fubmiffion and obe-dience to their lawful authority; not confidering them-felves upon a footing of natural equality with thofe whofe Slaves they are, though entitled at the fame time

time to all the promifes and fpiritual franchifes of true
Believers.

XII. From the tenour of thefe Apoftolic inftructions, confirmed by many other fimilar declarations to
the fame effect, frequently occurring in the Writings
of the New Teftament, I am naturally led to deduce
the following confequences in fupport of the licitnefs
of the SLAVE-TRADE.

1. IT is then evident from the Doctrine of St. Paul,
that Chriftians, however entitled by Baptifm to the
Spiritual freedom of Children of God, and Heirs of
heaven, ought yet, when under the yoke of human
bondage or flavery, confider themfelves under the
ftricteft obligation of reverencing the authority of their
Mafters, even of unbelieving Mafters, *and counting
them worthy of all honour*. But were the SLAVE-TRADE,
or the keeping of our fellow-creatures in bondage,
unnatural and unjuft, it could never be faid, that
Slaves were under the leaft obligation in confcience to
reverence and obey an unjuft, an unnatural authority;
or that their Mafters, who, by reducing them to that
abject condition, had trampled on the Sacred rights
of juftice and humanity, were *worthy of all honour*,
or, indeed, of any fhadow of honour, but, on the
contrary, of all difhonour and reproach.

2. IT is likewife evident from the Apoftle's doctrine, that the primitive Chriftians were not only not
forbidden, but exprefsly allowed by the principles of
our Religion the purchafing of Slaves, and keeping
their fellow-creatures, nay, even their fellow-Chriftians, under the yoke of bondage or Slavery ; and from
the circumftance of their Slaves being fo particularly
cautioned not to confider themfelves on the footing of
natural equality with their Mafters, not to defpife
them and their authority for being their equals in all
fpiritual attainments and franchifes, but to fhow, on
                                                    this

this very account, a greater degree of readinefs and
alacrity to render them due fervice, their Mafters are
evidently declared to have had a juft and indifputable
claim to that fervice, as their own lawful property.

XIII. NEITHER can it be faid, that this doctrine,
perhaps, novel to fome of my Readers, which Timothy is directed *to teach and to exhort*, was only the
private opinion of St. Paul; for he declares to him in
exprefs words, that it is *a doctrine according to godlinefs*, the very doctrine of Chrift himfelf, and not to
be contradicted by any one, without incurring the ac-
cumulated guilt of pride and folly with a criminal
train of attendants: " If any man, *fays be*, teach orher-
" wife, and confent not to wholefome words, even the
" words of our LORD JESUS CHRIST, and to the doc-
" trine, which is according to godlineis, he is proud,
" knowing nothing, but doting about queftions, and
" ftrifes of words, whereof cometh envy, ftrife, rail-
" ings, evil furmifings, &c."

XIV. So far then from being true, that there is nothing
in the Sacred Writings of the New Teftament, that
can be produced in vindication of the SLAVE-TRADE,
the palpable evidence juft produced in juftification of
that Trade from the authentic words of One of the
very principal infpired Authors of thofe Sacred Writings, muft convince every candid inquirer into the
merits of the prefent Controverfy, that, if the SLAVE-
TRADE, as demonftrated in the two preceding Parts,
appears fo vifibly warranted by the Writings of the Old
Teftament, the fame is not lefs evidently authorized,
but rather more explicitly vindicated from every fufpi-
cion of guilt and immorality by the Writings of the
New: for, they do not only declare in formal words,
that the teaching of the licitnefs of the SLAVE-TRADE,
exemplified in the practice of the Primitive Chriftians,
is a *Doctrine according to Godlinefs*, and according to
wholefome

wholefome words, even the words of our LORD JESUS
CHRIST, but they even ftigmatize the Teachers of the
contrary doctrine with epithets and appellations not of
the moft pleafing founds.

EPISTLE TO *PHILEMON.*

XV. PHILEMON, to whom St. Paul addreffes this
affectionate Epiftle, was a rich Coloffian, and a Chriftian of diftinguifhed merit. The character given of
him in the firft part of this Epiftle, reprefents him as
one of the moft zealous and fervent Chriftians of his
time. His affiduity in promoting the intereft of Chriftianity in quality of *Fellow-labourer* with St. Paul (*e*),
his *love and faith towards the Lord Jefus,* and his ge-
nerous unbounded charity *towards all the faints,* or his
fellow-Chriftians (*f*), whom he relieved and comfort-
ed on all occafions (*g*), gained him the confidence,
efteem, and affection of the Apoftle and of the whole
Church at large (*h*).

XVI. THIS Primitive and exemplary Chriftian had
in his fervice one ONESIMUS, a Slave, who, as it is
very ftrongly intimated by St. Paul, having defrauded
his Mafter of fome part of his property, and knowing
the influence the Apoftle had over him, eloped from
his Mafter's houfe, went to Rome, where St. Paul was
then in prifon, was converted by him, and received
into the Communion of the Chriftian Church (*i*); and
having by his good fervices and chriftian conduct,
gained the Apoftle's favour, he feems to have prevailed
on him to write to his Mafter Philemon in his behalf.

XVII. THE Letter, of which ONESIMUS himfelf appears to have been the Bearer, is a mafter-piece of
eloquence, and one of the fineft Compofitions extant
in the Epiftolary kind. Nothing can be more tender,

I   more

(*e*) Ep. to Phil. v. 1. (*f*) Ibid. v. 5. (*g*) Ibid. v. 7.
(*h*) Ibid. v. 7. (*i*) Ibid. v. 10.

more preſſing, more animated and perſuaſive : entrea-
ties and authority, praiſes and recommendations, religious motives and motives of perſonal gratitude and
integrity, are moſt inimitably well tempered and al-
layed together. In ſhort; almoſt every word of this
very conciſe Epiſtle contains ſome argument or reaſon
to effect a reconciliation between Philemon and Oneſimus, and to obtain from the Maſter the readmiſſion
of his fugitive Slave into his houſe and ſervice.

XVIII. The following XIV Verſes of this elegant
Epiſtle, which ſeem to have a more immediate con-
nexion than the reſt with the ſubject of our preſent inquiry, will afford me ſufficient matter for ſuch reflections, as will not only confirm the doctrine enforced
in this Section reſpecting the moral conformity of the
Slave-Trade with the principles of the Chriſtian Diſ-
penſation, but prevent me from proceeding any farther
in my Scriptural Researches on this intereſting
ſubject.

The following is a literal tranſcript of the Contents
of the Apoſtle's Letter to Philemon from the VIII th
to the XXII d Verſe.

8. Wherefore, though I might be much bold in
Chriſt to enjoin thee that which is convenient;

9. Yet, for love's ſake, I rather beſeech thee, being
ſuch a one as Paul the aged, and now alſo a priſoner
of Jeſus Chriſt.

10. I beſeech thee for my ſon Oneſimus, whom I
have begotten in my bonds.

11. Which in time paſt was to thee unprofitable;
but now profitable to thee and to me :

12. Whom I have ſent again : thou therefore receive him, that is mine own bowels.

13. Whom I would have retained with me, that in
thy ſtead he might have miniſtered unto me in the
bonds of the Goſpel.

14. But

14. But without thy mind would I do nothing, that thy benefit fhould not be, as it were, of neceffity, but willingly.

15. For perhaps he therefore departed for a feafon, that thou fhouldeft receive him for ever:

16. Not now as a fervant, but above a fervant, a brother beloved, efpecially to me, but how much more unto thee, both in the fleſh and in the Lord?

17. If thou count me therefore a partner, receive him as myfelf.

18. If he hath wronged thee, or oweth thee aught, put that on mine account.

19. I Paul have written it with my own hand, I will repay it: albeit I do not fay to thee, how thou oweft unto me even thine own felf befides:

20. Yea, Brother, let me have joy of thee in the Lord; refreſh my bowels in the Lord.

21. Having confidence in thy obedience, I wrote unto thee, knowing that thou wilt alfo do more than I fay.

XIX. The following obvious remarks, adapted to the fubject of our prefent inquiry refpecting the moral licitnefs of the SLAVE-TRADE, feem naturally to arife from the tenour of this facred portion of Scripture.

1. The Apoftle declares in the firft place, that, were he to act in the plenitude of his Apoftolic Commiffion and Authority, without any regard to the dictates of his love and friendſhip for Philemon, he would not ufe the ftyle of a fuppliant, as he does, but would peremptorily enjoin him to receive his fugitive Slave into his houfe and fervice, which he is bound to do in decency and duty: the word *Convenient* in the Original has both thefe meanings. From which declaration it evidently follows, that the Apoftle was fo far from thinking, that Philemon had acted wrong or unjuftly in keeping Onefimus in bondage, when yet an unbe-

liever,

liever, that he affures him, on the contrary, he would act in oppofition to his duty, or unjuftly, in not receiving him again, when baptized, into his houfe and fervice.

2. This declaration acquires a fuperior degree of force from the circumftance he fubjoins to his requeft, as a powerful inducement for Philemon to receive him again into his fervice. This circumftance, alluding to the name of ONESIMUS, which in Greek is the fame as PROFITABLE, is both beautiful and interefting. The Apoftle owns without difguife, that Onefimus *in time paft had* certainly *been an unprofitable*, or, in Scripture-language, *a bad Servant* (*k*): but, as he could now affure Philemon, that he was quite reclaimed, and become *profitable* to both, he earneftly folicits his read-miffion, in order that he may be enabled to make amends for his paft negligence and inattention to his fervice by his future diligence and affiduity.—It was then Onefimus's duty to have been ufeful and *profitable* to his Mafter Philemon, whilft under the yoke of fervitude; and it was an act of manifeft injuftice in him to have been *unprofitable* and of no fervice. Philemon then had a juft and undoubted right to the fervice of Onefimus, as his Slave; or elfe Onefimus could never have been taxed by the Apoftle with acting the part of an *unprofitable* or *bad fervant*, or with any perfonal injuftice, for neglecting a fervice, which Philemon had no right or title to demand.

3. Again: to convince Philemon, how much Onefimus was changed for the better fince his elopement, and the great reformation that his converfion to Chriftianity had wrought in his morals and conduct, he tells him, how much he was inclined himfelf to keep him in his own fervice; intimating to him in this delicate and gentle

(*k*) Matt. c. 25. v. 30

gentle manner, that he could have no objection to receive again into his fervice a perfon fo well qualified,
as Onefimus was then, to be an Apoftle's Servant: and
he affures him further, that the only reafon that has
prevented him from indulging his inclination to detain
him, has been his not having had his leave and confent for fo doing; *without which*, fays he, he would
never attempt to deprive him of his Slave.—From this
declaration it appears in the ftrongeft light, how very
facred and inviolable the acquired rights of Mafters
over their Slaves, even of Chriftian Mafters and Slaves,
were held by St. Paul, who would not by any means
deprive Philemon of Onefimus, however ufeful the
latter was to him at that time, and whatever afcen-
dency he had over his Mafter, without having firft
obtained his exprefs approbation and confent : he
would then, fays he, receive Onefimus, as a *benefit*
perfectly gratuitous, as a free and voluntary gift made
to him by Philemon of fo valuable a part of his
property.

4. Till he obtains this confent, he fends Onefimus
back to his lawful Mafter, entreating him in the moft
preffing and affectionate manner, to ufe him with all
poffible tendernefs and regard : to confider him now
as a member of the Communion of the true believers,
and confequently not in the character of a common
menial Slave, but as his own brother in Chrift, though
ftill his property *according to the flefh*, which to him
particularly ought to be dearer than ever, as being
now confecrated to God. — And left Philemon fhould
infift on Onefimus making due fatisfaction for having
defrauded him of his time, or other property, and
fhould, on that account, ufe him with feverity, the
Apoftle engages to make him full reparation, and becomes himfelf refponfible for the whole : which is a
manifeft

manifeſt acknowledgement of Philemon's right, as the lawful Maſter of Oneſimus, to inflict due puniſhment on his SLAVE.

XX. FROM theſe obſervations, ſo naturally flowing from the Contents of the Apoſtle's letter to Philemon, theſe two neceſſary conſequences ſeem as naturally to follow.

1. Had St. Paul, who had been inſtructed in the principles of the Chriſtian Religion, not by men, but immediately by Chriſt himſelf (*l*), *whoſe choſen veſſel he was to bear his name before the Gentiles, and Kings, and the Children of Iſrael (*m*)*, been taught by his Divine Maſter, that the SLAVE-TRADE, or the purchaſing of Slaves, or keeping thoſe already purchaſed in ſervitude or bondage, was an unnatural, iniquitous purſuit, contrary to the Spirit of his Religion, he would have certainly addreſſed himſelf to Philemon in a very different ſtyle from that of his preſent Letter ; and, inſtead of acting the part of a Suppliant, the part of an interceſſor and Mediator, as he does, in ſoliciting of him the re-admiſſion of a fugitive Slave, he would have aſſumed the ſtyle and tone of a Maſter ; would have ſeverely condemned the unjuſtifiable conduct of Philemon in detaining him in criminal bondage, contrary to the Laws of his holy Religion, would have commended the ſpirited conduct of Oneſimus in ſhaking off the heavy yoke of ſervitude, would not have ſuffered him to return to his unnatural Maſter Philemon, eſpecially after he had converted him to Chriſtianity, and entitled him by Baptiſm to the glorious franchiſes and liberty of the Children of God, and would not have ſtood on complimentary ceremonies, finding him uſeful in his actual ſtate of confinement,

(*l*) Galat, c. 1. v. 1.   (*m*) Acts, c. 9. v. 15.

ment, to retain him in his miniftry, without afking his pretended Mafter's leave, or without his confent.

THIS, I am confident, would have been the language and conduct of the Apoftle, had he been taught by his Divine Mafter, that the principles and doctrine of the Gofpel, he was commiffioned to preach, were in direct oppofition to the practice of the SLAVE-TRADE, to the practice of purchafing Slaves, or keeping thofe already purchafed in bondage or flavery.

2. But, fince the Apoftle, conformably to the inftructions he had received from his Lord and Mafter JESUS CHRIST, refpecting every part of a Chriftian's duty, expreffes himfelf in this Epiftle, as well as in every other, where he fpeaks on this much mifreprefented fubject, in terms and language diametrically oppofite to the fentiments juft mentioned; we are forced to conclude, that, fince Philemon, as well as many other Primitive Chriftians, cotemporary with the Apoftles of Chrift and firft Teachers of Chriftianity, kept Slaves, even Chriftian Slaves, in their fervice, in the very face of the whole Church, and with the approbation and knowledge of the primitive Apoftles and Difciples of Chrift, as has been demonftrated from fome of the cleareft teftimonies of the New Teftament, the nature of the SLAVE-TRADE, being fo vifibly authorized by the pofitive fanction of thofe Sacred Writings, muft be effentially juft and lawful in its principles, and perfectly confonant to thofe of the Chriftian Law.

XXI. EVIDENT as this conclufion appears from the Scriptural arguments enforced in the courfe of this SECTION, I cannot clofe the Subject of thefe RESEARCHES without taking fome notice of what, I apprehend, will be objected againft it from the Words of our Bleffed Saviour in his divine Sermon on the Mount, which in the VIII th Number of this Section I declared with

particular

particular ſtreſs to contain nothing againſt the licitneſs
of the SLAVE-TRADE.— The Words, here alluded to,
will, I preſume, be thus retorted againſt it.

All things whatſoever, ſays our Bleſſed Saviour, *ye
would that men ſhould do to you, do ye even ſo to them ;
for this is the Law and the Prophets (n) :* whatſoever
things therefore we would not, that men ſhould do to
us, we are not even ſo to do to them ; but no perſon
whatever would certainly wiſh, that a fellow-creature
ſhould reduce him to the condition of a Slave ; therefore no perſon whatever is to reduce a fellow-creature
to that condition.

XXII. HERE again I muſt obſerve, that no one can
juſtly tax me with any partiality to the Cauſe I have
eſpouſed: I have, I think, worded the argument againſt
it in terms as forcible, as the moſt zealous advocate
for African Liberty, could uſe. But unanſwerable as
the ſame may appear to them, it is but a plauſible
argument at the beſt.

IT is an Axiom in LOGIC, that *An argument that
proves too much, proves nothing :* the above is juſt ſuch
a one : for, by the ſame manner of reaſoning, one
might equally conclude, contrary to the Law and the
Prophets, and the doctrine of the Chriſtian Religion,
that not only Slavery, but every other kind of ſubor-
dination of one man to another, ought not to be ſuffered to continue in the World. — The argument, if
concluſive in the former caſe, muſt be equally ſo in
the latter : I enforce it thus : —

All things whatſoever, ſays our Bleſſed Saviour, *ye would
that men ſhould do to you, do ye even ſo to them ; for this
is the Law and the Prophet*s : whatſoever things therefore we would not that men ſhould do to us, we are
not even ſo to do to them ; but every perſon would naturally

(n) Matt. c. 7. v. 12.

turally with not to be controlled by a fellow-creature, not to be under any fubjection to him, but to be abfolute mafter of his own actions; no perfon therefore ought to keep a fellow-creature under any control or fubjection whatever.

XXIII. Such is the confequence of wrefting the natural and obvious meaning of the maxims of Scripture, and applying them to purpofes inconfiftent with Scripture itfelf. The Golden Maxim of our Divine Mafter, comprehending in two words the whole perfection of a Chriftian, was certainly intended by him for all ftations in life, for of fuch was his Church to confift to the end of time: from the Throne to the Cottage, in every walk of life, in bondage or at liberty, every Chriftian is taught and directed To do unto others, as he would be done unto; and, by a neceffary confequence Not to do unto others, as he would not be done unto: that is, every Chriftian is commanded to behave to his neighbour, in whatever fituation or circumftances in life Providence may have placed them both, juft as he would wifh his neighbour would behave to him in his fituation, were his neighbour's fituation and circumftances his own: fo that, to apply the Maxim to a particular Cafe (even the Cafe in queftion), no Chriftian Mafter can be faid *to do unto others as he would be done unto*, unlefs he behaves to his Slave with the fame tendernefs, juftice, and humanity, as he would wifh his Slave would behave to him, were the Slave his Mafter, and himfelf the Slave; and, upon the fame principle, no Slave can be faid *to do unto others as he would be done unto*, unlefs he ferves his Mafter with the fame fidelity, fubmiffion, and refpect, which he would expect from his Mafter, were the latter his Slave, and himfelf the Mafter.

K

XXIV. The

XXIV. The Golden Maxim then, of Doing unto Others, as we would be done unto, is so far from condemning in the most distant manner the profecution of the Slave-Trade, that, when applied to the Cafe of Chriftian Mafters and their Slaves, it ferves, on the contrary, to enforce their reciprocal duties in their different fpheres of life. Neither could it be otherwife, feeing, that the fame Divine Authority, on which the truth of the above Maxim is founded, has fo frequently given his fanction in the Writings of both the Teftaments to the licitnefs of the Slave-Trade.

XXV. I have now, I think, verified in its full extent the Affertion I engaged to prove in the Title-page; that thefe Scriptural Researches on the licitnefs of the Slave-Trade, would fhew the moral conformity of that Trade with the Principles of Natural and Revealed Religion delineated in the Sacred Writings of the Word of God: and as I prefixed to the Whole certain Pofitions or Data, on the truth of which the undeniable religious certainty of that moral conformity is entirely founded, fo I fhall now annex to the whole a few Corollaries or Confequences, which, from their neceffary dependance on the former Data, muft convince every religious and candid Reader of the neceffity of acquiefcing in the Scriptural Doctrine enforced in thefe Researches.

COROLLARIES.

COROLLARIES.

I.

SINCE the Sacred Writings of the HOLY BIBLE contain the unerring Decisions of the WORD of GOD, the Authority of which in both the Teftaments is founded on the effential veracity of God, who is TRUTH itfelf; it follows neceffarily, that, as there can be no prefcription againft that Authority, which, in the feveral fcriptural paffages quoted in the feries of the foregoing RESEARCHES, has pofitively declared, that the SLAVE-TRADE is intrinfically good and licit, this, by a neceffary confequence, muft be effentially fo in its own nature, however contrary fuch declaration may be to the received opinion of fome men for any length of time.

II.

SINCE the Supreme Legiflator of the World is infinitely juft and wife in all his Decifions refpecting *Right* and *Wrong*, and is no ways accountable to his Creatures for the reafons of his conduct in the government of the World; fo it muft be a degree of prefumption highly criminal in any creature to refufe affent to thofe particular Decifions, by which he has fo pofitively declared the intrinfic licitnefs of the SLAVE-TRADE, only becaufe he cannot account for that impartial juftice, which characterizes every Decifion of God, from thofe hidden principles of Eternal Juftice, incomprehenfible to him, which induced the Almighty to eftablifh in the World that fubordinate ftate of abfolute fubjection of fome of his rational Creatures to others.

III.

SINCE no perfon can be fuppofed to acknowledge in fact, that the HOLY SCRIPTURES are the unerring

WORD

Word of God, unlefs he acquiefces without referve in every Scriptural Decifion, however incomprehenfible the reafons and motives of thofe Decifions may be to him, and that on no other account, but becaufe he believes them to be the Declarations of God, who, being Truth itfelf, can neither err himfelf, nor lead any one into error ; it follows neceffarily, that whoever does not acquiefce in thofe Scriptural Decifions, quoted in the feries of the foregoing Researches, declaring in formal Words the licitnefs of the Slave-Trade, cannot be faid to acknowledge in fact, that the Holy Scriptures are the unerring Word of God.

IV.

Since not only one, but feveral Decifions of the Written Word of God, as appears from the foregoing Researches, give a pofitive fanction to the licitnefs of the Slave-Trade; it is not from the principle of private or National advantages attending the profecution of it, which can never affect the intrinfic nature of any human purfuit, that any one is to believe, that the Slave-Trade is intrinfically juft and lawful in the ftricteft fenfe of the word, but from the incontrovertible veracity of the Written Word of God, whofe Decifions they are, and who is effentially incompatible with the leaft degree of injuftice.

V.

Since no abufes or malepractices whatever, committed in the profecution of a lawful purfuit, can ever alter the intrinfic licitnefs of it ; there being no other arguments, that can be produced againft the Slave-Trade, but fuch as are built on the ftrength of fuch abufes as are faid to be perpetrated in the profecution of it ; no arguments whatever will ever evince any intrinfic moral turpitude in its Nature, fo explicitly declared

clared juft and lawful in the Sacred Writings of the
Word of God, notwithftanding the many abufes to
which it was formerly fubjeƈt, and were formerly practifed, as well as now.

VI.

Since no abufes or malepraƈtices whatever, though
of the greateft magnitude, committed in former times
in the profecution of the Slave-Trade (*a*), ever induced the Almighty to prohibit or abolifh that Trade,
but only to check by wholefome and coercive Laws
the violence of unnatural Mafters (*b*), and to punifh
the tranfgreffors with the greateft feverity (*c*); there
appears no reafon whatever, why the abufes and malepraƈtices faid to be perpetrated in our days in the profecution of the fame Trade, evidently fubjeƈt to the
control of the Legiflature, fhould be deemed a powerful inducement to proceed to the abolition of it.

(*a*) Gen. 35. 22. Exod. 21. 8, 16, 20, 26, 27. Levit. 19. 20.
Jerem. 34. v. 8—18. (*b*) Exod. 21. v. 7, 12, 16, 20, 21,
26, 27. Levit. 19. v. 20, 21, 22. Ibid. 25. v. 39—43.
(*c*) Jeremiah, c. 34. v. 17—22.

ADVERTISEMENT.

ADVERTISEMENT.

IT was the Author's defign, when he firft engaged to vindicate the licitnefs of the SLAVE-TRADE from the Sacred Writings of the WORD of GOD, to have concluded his RESEARCHES with another SECTION, containing fome Scriptural Directions for the proper treatment of Slaves, together with fome Exemplary Punifhments and Comminations regiftered in the fame divine Repofitory of religious Knowledge, for deterring the Conductors and Proprietors of Slaves from ever infringing by any acts of violence and oppreffion the facred bounds of that Authority, with which they are entrufted for a time, and which they can never trefpafs with abfolute impunity : but the fhortnefs of the time, which his other avocations have allowed him for completing the Scriptural Vindication contained in the three Sections of his RESEARCHES, having made it abfolutely impoffible for him to execute the whole of his Original Defign, he is obliged to offer it to the Public in its prefent ftate.

E R R A T A.

Page 21, line 7, whaterer, *read* whatever.

Page 30, line 23, four or five, *read* ten.

Page 35, line 23, fale, *read* fell.

Page 42, line 7, among, *read* among them.

Page 47, line 23, wole, *read* whole.

Page 48, line 24, unjuft, *read* juft.

www.ingramcontent.com/pod-product-compliance
Lightning Source LLC
Chambersburg PA
CBHW022143090426
42742CB00010B/1373